Fostering Business Development and Digitalisation in Georgia

OECD

This work is published under the responsibility of the Secretary-General of the OECD. The opinions expressed and arguments employed herein do not necessarily reflect the official views of the Member countries of the OECD.

This document, as well as any data and map included herein, are without prejudice to the status of or sovereignty over any territory, to the delimitation of international frontiers and boundaries and to the name of any territory, city or area.

Please cite this publication as:
OECD (2022), *Fostering Business Development and Digitalisation in Georgia*, OECD Publishing, Paris, https://doi.org/10.1787/c6e27d8a-en.

ISBN 978-92-64-82063-0 (print)
ISBN 978-92-64-46657-9 (pdf)
ISBN 978-92-64-70714-6 (HTML)
ISBN 978-92-64-33152-5 (epub)

Foreword

The Government of Georgia has made significant policy efforts over the past years to build an environment conducive to private sector development and entrepreneurship, and to support small and medium-sized enterprises in particular. The OECD has supported this reform impetus, working closely with the Ministry of Economy and Sustainable Development (MoESD) to help identify gaps and develop relevant measures to create a conducive policy environment for Georgian SMEs. Georgia participated and featured as top improver in the three rounds of Small Business Act assessment for the Eastern Partner countries, which resulted in the corresponding OECD publications *SME Policy Index: Eastern Partner countries* 2012, 2016 and 2020. In parallel, at country-level, the OECD supported the design of Georgia's SME development strategy 2016-2020, and assessed the progress made in the implementation in 2018. As a follow-up to this work and upon request of the MoESD, the OECD provided assistance in preparing the new SME Development Strategy 2021-2025 ("the Strategy" hereafter) and the related Action Plan for the first implementation period, building on the findings of the latest SME Policy Index (OECD et al., 2020[1]).

This project was carried out as part of *EU4Business: From Policies to Action*, a multi-country project carried out by the OECD with the financial support of the European Union, and in close cooperation with the European Union and GIZ. The MoESD established a dedicated public-private working group to elaborate the Strategy, which gathered on several occasions throughout 2020-2021, including two working group meetings organised in September 2020 and March 2021 to discuss challenges and reform priorities for SMEs in Georgia. The OECD also provided support in costing the measures of the first Action Plan through three dedicated technical workshops, during which members of the working group discussed the costing methodology and worked on concrete examples taken from the draft Strategy's Action Plan. The final version of the Strategy was approved mid July 2021 by the Government of Georgia.

While this work was conducted under phase 1 of the *EU4Business: From Policies to Action* project, phase 2 of the EU4Business project launched in May 2021 aims at helping Eastern Partner countries "build back better" with a strong emphasis on supporting the digitalisation of SMEs. In that context and as an immediate follow-up to the work on the Strategy, the OECD is helping the Government of Georgia to design policies to accelerate the digital transformation of SMEs. In that regard, two working group meetings took place in June and October 2021, gathering senior policymakers from Georgia, private sector representatives and international practitioners and experts from OECD countries, as well as EU and OECD representatives.

This peer review note is the result of these two work-streams:

- the first part summarises the assessment and recommendations provided for the SME Strategy, highlighting the measures that have been implemented and the additional steps that could be considered for future action plans over the implementation period;
- the second part is dedicated to SME digitalisation in Georgia, taking stock of the current state of play in terms of both framework conditions and dedicated support programmes for SME digitalisation, and providing policy options to accelerate the digital transformation of SMEs.

This note served as a basis for discussion for at a peer review of Georgia at the OECD Eurasia Competitiveness Roundtable (November 2021).

Acknowledgements

This report summarises the work carried out by the OECD Eurasia Competitiveness Programme (ECP) under the authority of the OECD Eastern Europe and South Caucasus Initiative Steering Committee, in consultation with the Government of Georgia and with participation of private sector and international organisations in Georgia. The project component on "Designing Georgia's SME Development Strategy 2021-2025" was implemented in close co-operation with the European Union and GIZ Georgia.

Representatives of several Georgian ministries, government agencies, private sector associations, non-governmental organisations and other stakeholders should be acknowledged for their active participation in working group meetings and their availability to exchange with the OECD team and share valuable insights for the development of this note.

In particular, the OECD would like to extend its gratitude to the following representatives of the Ministry of Economy and Sustainable Development: Ekaterine Mikabadze (former Deputy Minister), Guram Guramishvili and Irakli Nadareishvili (Deputy Ministers), Tsisnami Sabadze (Head of Economic Policy Department), Eka Kubusidze (Head of Telecommunications, Information and Modern Technologies Department), and Giorgi Dapkviashvili (Head of Electronic Communications and Information Technologies Development Division).

The OECD is also very grateful to other representatives of the Government of Georgia, government agencies and other public institutions for their important contributions to the project, notably to Tamar Kitiashvili (Deputy Minister of Education, Science, Culture and Sport); Mikhail Khidureli (CEO), Tornike Zirakishvili (Deputy Director), Irakli Gabriadze (Deputy Director), all three from Enterprise Georgia; Avtandil Kasradze (Chairman, Georgia's Innovation and Technology Agency); and Eka Gordadze (Manager of Digital Governance and Cyber Security Strategic Directions, Digital Governance Agency).

The report, as well as working group discussions, benefitted from very insightful inputs by representatives of the private sector: Nana Tsertsvadze (Deputy CEO of the Business Association of Georgia), Magda Bolotashvili (Deputy General Director, Georgian Chamber of Commerce and Industry), Gvantsa Meladze (Supervisory Board Member, Export Development Association (EDA)), and Nino Elizbarashvili (Georgian Association Women in Business).

A number of international experts provided valuable contributions to the report and working group discussions, including Janez Šušteršič (expert on monitoring, evaluation and costing), Jesus Lozano (IT entrepreneur and senior expert on SME digitalisation), and, from GIZ Georgia, Hans-Jürgen Cassens (Programme Director), Philipp Steinheim (Team Leader, Clusters4Development), Marina Avalishvili-de Boer (Programme expert) , Selma Ulrichs (Team Leader Georgia), and Ketevan Gorgoshidze (former Co-ordinator of costing of SME Action Plan). Some of the working group meetings saw the participation of additional experts, including Isae Spinu (Head of SMEs digitalisation and IT support, Organisation for SME Sector Development of Moldova) and Elif Koksal-Oudot (Economist, OECD Directorate for Science, Technology and Innovation).

The European Union provided financial support for this project as part of the EU4Business initiative. Hoa-Binh Adjemian (Head of Sector, Economic Development), Michaela Hauf (former Team Leader for

Georgia), and Michael Rupp (current Team Leader for Georgia), all from DG NEAR, European Commission, and Dominik Papenheim (Team Leader, Economic Development and Market opportunities, Budget Support Co-ordination, Delegation of the European Union to Georgia) provided important guidance and support for this project.

This report was written under the guidance of Andreas Schaal, Director of the OECD Global Relations Secretariat, and William Tompson, Head of the OECD Eurasia Division.

The project was managed by Daniel Quadbeck, Senior Policy Analyst and Head of the Eastern European and South Caucasus Unit, and Francesco Alfonso, Economist and Deputy Head of Unit, both from the OECD Eurasia Division.

The main author of this report is Salomé Will, with valuable support provided by Anna-Maria Ghersi (both OECD Eurasia Division).

The report was reviewed by Jorge Gálvez Mendéz (Economist in the OECD Directorate for Financial and Enterprise Affairs) and Gerhard Laga (Head of e-Center and *SME Digital Initiative* at the Austrian Economic Chamber), and benefitted from additional inputs by Krzysztof Michalak (Senior Programme Manager) and Guy Halpern (Policy Analyst) both from the OECD Environment Directorate.

Very valuable administrative support was provided by Eugenia Klimenka, Mariana Tanova and Elisa Larrakoetxea (OECD Eurasia Division).

Table of contents

Figures

Boxes

Acronyms and abbreviations

AI	Artificial intelligence
API	Application Programme Interfaces
ASEAN	Association of Southeast Asian Nations
BAG	Business Association of Georgia
BfD	Broadband-for-Development
CERT	Computer Emergency Response Team
CICs	Community Innovation Centres
CIS	Commonwealth of Independent States
ComCom	Communications Commission
COSME	Competitiveness of Enterprises and Small and Medium-sized Enterprises
CRM	Customer Relationship Management
DCFTA	Deep and Comprehensive Free Trade Area
DGA	Digital Governance Agency
EAD	Early Warning Denmark
EaP	Eastern Partnership
EaPeReg	Eastern Partnership Electronic Communications Regulators Network
EBRD	European Bank for Reconstruction and Development
eID	Electronic Identity
eIDAS	Electronic Identification, Authentication and trust Services
ERP	Enterprise Resource Planning
EU	European Union
EUR	Euro
FabLabs	Fabrication Laboratories
FDI	Foreign Direct Investment
FFE	Federation of Finnish Enterprises
FinTech	Financial Technology
GCCI	Georgian Chamber of Commerce and Industry

GCI	Global Cybersecurity Index
GDP	Gross Domestic Product
GDPR	General Data Protection Regulation
GEL	Georgian Lari
GENIE	Georgia National Innovation Ecosystem
GITA	Georgia's Innovation and Technology agency
GIZ	Deutsche Gesellschaft für Internationale Zusammenarbeit [German Corporation for International Cooperation]
GNBA	Georgian National Blockchain Agency
GNCC	Georgian National Communications Commission
GoG	Government of Georgia
GRENA	Georgian Research And Educational Networking Association
GSMEA	Georgian Small and Medium Enterprises Association
GUAM	Organisation for Democracy and Economic Development
ICT	Information and Communication Technology
IMF	International Monetary Fund
INFE	International Network on Financial Education
INSEAD	Institut Européen d'Administration des Affaires
IoT	Internet of Things
ISOC	Internet Society
IT	Information Technology
ITU	International Telecommunication Union
KISA	Korea's Internet Security Agency
KMU	Kleine und Mittlere Unternehmen [Small and Medium Enterprises]
KPI	Key Performance Indicators
LEPL	Legal Entity under Public law
LMIS	Labour Market Information Systems
MENA	Middle East and North Africa region
MoESD	Georgian Ministry of Economy and Sustainable Development
MSME	Micro Small and Medium Enterprises
NATO	North Atlantic Treaty Organization
NBDS	National Broadband Development Strategy
NBG	National Bank of Georgia
NIS	Network and Information Systems
NLP	Natural Language Processing

NRA	National Regulatory Authority
ODIMM	Organizaţia pentru Dezvoltarea Sectorului Întreprinderilor Mici şi Mijlocii [Moldova's Organisation for the Development of Small and Medium Enterprises Sector]
OECD	Organisation for Economic Co-operation and Development
OSCE	Organization for Security and Co-operation in Europe
PPD	Public-Private Dialogues
PPE	Personal Protective Equipment
R&D	Research and Development
RFID	Radio Frequency Identification
RIA	Regulatory Impact Assessment
RIH	Regional Innovation Hubs
SaaS	Software as a Service
SARAS	Service for Accounting, Reporting and Auditing Supervision
SCM	Supply Chain Management
SDA	Public Service Development Agency
SELFIE	Self-reflection on Effective Learning by Fostering the use of Innovative Educational technologies
SME	Small and Medium-sized Enterprises
SMEPI	Small and Medium-sized Enterprises Policy Index
STEM	Science, Technology, Engineering and Mathematics
UN	United Nations
UNDP	United Nations Development program
US	United States
USAID	United States Aid
USD	United States Dollars
VET	Vocational education Training

Executive summary

Small and medium-sized enterprises (SMEs) play an important role in Georgia's economy, accounting for 65% of total employment and 59.3% of value added in 2019, up from 58.1% in 2015. However, they remain mostly concentrated in low-value-added sectors, and their productivity is still well below EU levels. Moreover, Georgian SMEs have been particularly affected by the COVID-19 crisis, notably because of their over-representation in hardly hit sectors such as services and tourism, and higher risk of liquidity shortages. By end 2020, some 5.4% of small and 2% of medium firms were reportedly permanently closed (against 0.4% of large ones), while 82% and 86% of small and medium firms, respectively, had experienced decreased liquidity or cash flow availability since the pandemic outbreak (against 68% of large firms). Dedicated and comprehensive policies for the SME sector are therefore needed, both to sustain a strong, inclusive, green and resilient recovery, as well as to further foster the development of the SME sector in the long run.

To this end, the OECD has assisted the Government of Georgia in designing policies based on the assessment of the current state of play, taking stock of the progress achieved and identifying remaining challenges to i) prepare Georgia's new SME Development Strategy 2021-2025 and its first related Action Plan, and ii) accelerate the digital transformation of SMEs.

Part 1 focuses on the work conducted on the SME Development Strategy 2021-2025 and its first Action Plan, providing an overview of the main issues identified by the OECD for each of the Strategy's seven dimensions, as well as policy recommendations for future action plans and key performance indicators (KPIs) to monitor implementation progress.

- Georgia has considerably improved its **institutional framework and operational environment**, e.g. through the expansion and formalisation of public-private participation in policymaking, fast-growing availability and use of e-government services, and the long-awaited reform of the insolvency framework. However, the spike in business failures resulting from the pandemic calls for actions to promote restructuring and entrepreneurial fresh starts. Awareness-raising initiatives on changing regulations could be stepped up to help SMEs keep track of new legislations, and SME statistics could be further broadened, using OECD databases as examples.

- Several steps have been taken to foster the development of **entrepreneurial skills and culture**, including the creation of a labour market information system, non-formal learning initiatives, and the introduction of entrepreneurship in national school curricula at all levels of education. Yet there is a persistent skills mismatch, and little co-operation between enterprises and Vocational Education Training (VET) institutions. Given the rise of economic lay-offs, Georgia could consider measures to help laid off workers transition to new jobs, strengthen industry/VET schools linkages, and foster digital skills development.

- **Access to finance** for Georgian SMEs is improving, thanks to more favourable credit conditions, measures to develop alternative bank financing, and initiatives to foster financial literacy (e.g. a dedicated National Strategy and guidebooks for entrepreneurs). Alternative and digital finance solutions could be further developed through the enhancement of the legal environment (e.g. regulatory sandboxes, legal definition of business angel, harmonisation with advanced EU Venture

Capital (VC) regulations, etc.). Further steps could also be taken to prepare for the post-COVID era, to adapt financial support instruments and address the risk of a solvency crisis.

- On **SME internationalisation**, SME exports have been increasing (+41% since 2015), which goes in line with improvements in the overall trade environment reflected in the *OECD Trade facilitation indicators*. However, exports remain mostly directed to neighbouring markets, little diversified and low value-added. Exports to the EU are increasing, but slower than exports towards neighbouring countries. More could be done to tackle persistent information barriers and improve knowledge of market opportunities and requirements (e.g. export help desks), reduce high shipping costs and delivery times to EU countries (e.g. warehousing options), and develop e-commerce. Trade financing options could also be considered to overcome specific financial barriers experienced by exporting companies.

- Georgia has strengthened its policy and legal framework for **innovation** by adopting a dedicated law and expanding its innovation infrastructures and financing tools. Yet spending on research and development remains well below OECD levels, and support for innovation in non-IT sectors is still limited. Moving forward, Georgia could introduce indirect financial incentives for innovation, demand-side policies, and financing tools targeted at supporting the digitalisation of non-IT sectors.

- The overall environment for **women entrepreneurs** has improved via the creation of a sub-committee on women entrepreneurship, the introduction of gender-sensitive measures in recently adopted laws, and the enhancement of women participation in support programmes. However, women still encounter more difficulties in accessing finance, and data show a persistent gender gap in employability and wages. Conducting regular studies on barriers to women entrepreneurship and awareness-raising activities could help tackle remaining stereotypes and issues.

- The Government is making increasing efforts to promote the **green economy** development through various policy documents, as well as green measures implemented in response to the pandemic. However, Georgia should adopt an overarching vision for green growth by setting concrete definitions and policy goals, and foresee measures tailored to SMEs, e.g. in terms of efficiency and awareness-raising. Tasking Enterprise Georgia with leading support for SME greening would help improve co-ordination and outreach.

Part 2 delves deeper into the topic of digitalisation, as the latter can be a driver of structural transformation for SMEs. Digital technologies can help increase SME productivity through easier access to strategic resources, broaden the customer base, achieve scale and capitalise on network effects. The potential of digitalisation remains however untapped, especially among SMEs whose levels of technology uptake lag behind that of large firms. The report assesses the current state of play in terms of framework conditions, such as broadband connectivity, the regulatory environment and digital literacy, and SME digitalisation, looking at past policy achievements and upcoming measures, and outlines policy recommendations for each of these aspects.

- Georgia has provided efforts to develop an **institutional and policy framework** for the digital transformation. Adopting a comprehensive National Digital Strategy would help define clear objectives and measures, and increase co-operation between stakeholders. In that regard, the Government of Georgia could task one of the existing SME agencies with leading support for SME digitalisation to increase policy efficiency and outreach.

- In terms of **framework conditions**, Georgia appears as one of the most connected countries of the Eastern Partnership. Affordability, especially of fixed broadband, and speed remain an issue. Fostering competition, investment and innovation while strengthening the demand-side could help. The legal and regulatory framework in place, enhanced by a national regulatory authority, would benefit from further harmonisation with EU standards and the adoption of a dedicated e-commerce legislation. Digital security and data protection could be improved by strengthening incident response capacities, stepping up dedicated initiatives and completing the legal framework. As for digital skills, Georgia has implemented several policy initiatives, but still lags behind EaP and OECD peers. Additional measures could be considered, such as conducting regular digital skills needs assessment and gathering all training initiatives in a single place.

- As for **support programmes targeted at SMEs**, Georgia has put considerable effort in supporting the emergence of "digital-by-default" firms, through both financial and non-financial tools (e.g. infrastructure development, training, and networking). Yet initiatives for the digital transformation of "traditional" sectors are relatively scarce. This Note provides a blueprint to fill this gap, suggesting policy options to raise awareness of the benefits of digitalisation, enable firms to carry out a diagnosis of their digital maturity and needs, provide tailored financial and non-financial solutions, and ensure coordination and cooperation within the digitalisation ecosystem.

Summary of recommendations: way forward

Part of the report	Strategic direction	Way forward
Part 1: Recommendations for Georgia's SME development strategy 2021-2025	Strengthening the institutional framework and operational environment for SMEs	• Promote restructuring and entrepreneurial fresh start • Apply an SME test in the process of adopting new regulations • Step up awareness-raising initiatives on changing regulations for SMEs • Conduct impact evaluation of government-sponsored programmes • Broaden statistics on SMEs
	Fostering the development of entrepreneurial skills and raising the entrepreneurial culture of SMEs	• Use re-skilling programmes to help laid-off workers transition to new jobs • Strengthen industry/VET schools linkages • Foster the development of online-based solutions for VET modules • Adopt a comprehensive approach to develop digital skills
	Improving access to finance	• Adapt COVID-19-related financial support packages to the post-crisis period • Strengthen the legal environment for alternative and digital financing instruments • Further develop VC and business angels ecosystem • Broaden financial education initiatives
	Promoting export growth, market access and SME internationalisation	• Support SMEs in identifying market opportunities • Increase advisory and training to improve knowledge of market requirements • Help reduce SME shipping cost and time • Consider expanding use of trade financing options • Develop e-commerce skills and practices

Part of the report	Strategic direction	Way forward
	Supporting ICT adoption, innovation and R&D for SMEs	• Provide indirect financial incentives for innovation • Introduce financing tools supporting the digital transformation in non-IT sectors • Consider demand-side policies • Deepen research/industry linkages
	Encouraging women's entrepreneurship	• Develop gender-tailored support programmes • Improve data collection on gender-related issues • Step up awareness-raising activities
	Developing the green economy	• Set more concrete definitions and goals in the Strategy document • Task Enterprise Georgia with leading support for SME greening • Target efficiency measures to SMEs • Build capacity and awareness of opportunities from green economy
Part 2: Accelerating the digital transformation of SMEs	Institutional and policy setting for digitalisation	• Adopt National Digital Strategy with clearly defined objectives, actions and resources • Task one of existing SME support agencies with leading support for digitalisation
	Framework conditions for digitalisation	• Ensure broadband connectivity of higher quality and at lower prices • Harmonise regulatory framework with EU standards to allow for more interoperability and exchanges with the EU market • Enhance digital security to build trust in the digital economy • Foster digital skills development
	Develop comprehensive support for the digitalisation of non-IT sectors	• Raise awareness of benefits of digitalisation and build a digital culture among SMEs • Enable firms to carry out a diagnosis of their digital maturity and needs assessment • Provide SMEs with non-financial solutions tailored to their needs • Increase financial support options for the digitalisation of "traditional" firms • Ensure coordination and cooperation within the digitalisation ecosystem

Introduction

Economic context

The Georgian economy had been experiencing steady growth since 2015, up to the outbreak of the COVID-19 pandemic in 2020. GDP growth rose from below 3% in 2015 and 2016 to 4.8% y-o-y in 2017, and stabilized around 5% in the following years (Table 0.1). Exports of goods and services have reached 54.8% of GDP in 2019, compared to 40.8% in 2015. In particular, exports towards the EU have risen since the application of the EU-Georgia Deep and Comprehensive Free Trade Area (DCFTA) in 2014, reaching 24.2% of total exports in 2019 (German Economic Team, 2019[2]). Although this increase was accompanied by a diversification of exported goods, with a growth of processed goods, the main export basis has remained low value added, limiting the export potential (Economic Intelligence Unit, 2019[3]). The current account deficit has been reducing, while FDI stock increased to up to 100% in 2018.

The Government of Georgia (GoG) has conducted a set of reforms in recent years, which included a long-awaited reform of the framework for insolvency (further detailed in Part 1), a modernisation of the labour code, and continued efforts to foster infrastructure development and integration in global value chains. Moreover, within the framework of an extended fund facility signed with the IMF in 2017, the government has adopted a second-pillar pension reform. These policy efforts have led to significant improvements in the business environment, as reflected by Georgia's position in international assessments: Georgia ranks 12th out of 180 countries in the Heritage Foundation's *2021 Index of Economic Freedom*, scoring higher than the European and World averages. Since 2016, the country has gained eleven positions, thanks to improvements in judicial effectiveness, labour freedom and fiscal policy (Heritage Foundation, 2021[4]). Georgia ranks 5th out of 162 countries in the Fraser Institute's *Economic Freedom of the World 2021* and 74th out of 141 countries in the World Economic Forum's *Global Competitiveness Index 2019* thanks to its business enabling environment, ICT adoption, labour market and future workforce skills.

However, several challenges remain. Georgia still suffers from high level of unemployment, stagnating at about 20% over the period 2015-2020 (down to 18.5% in 2020), and of poverty, which still affects nearly 20% of the Georgian population. Moreover, the country still entails a large rural population (about 41% in 2020) and informal economy. The skills mismatch is also a persistent issue, although the Government has tried to tackle it by introducing a comprehensive educational reform in 2019, which has been partially stalled by the pandemic (IMF, 2021[5]). The productivity levels remain relatively low, albeit increasing, and regional interconnectivity is still limited.

Moreover, the country has been severely hit by the COVID-19 pandemic: despite its initial success in limiting new infections during the first wave, Georgia recorded a surge in daily new cases during the following waves, becoming one of the most affected countries in the world on a per capita basis, both in terms of deaths and cases. Vaccination is slowly advancing, with international community aid providing additional doses of vaccines, but is still at low rates (23% of the population had been fully vaccinated by mid-September 2021). During the successive waves, the government has enacted a range of containment measures to limit the spread of the virus, which have taken a toll on the economy (OECD, 2020[6]). The Georgian GDP decreased by 6.2% in 2020. This is partially explained by the shock to the service sector, notably tourism, which holds a prominent place in the Georgian economy – services exports dropped by 63.5% in 2020. Unemployment and poverty significantly rose from the previous year despite the mitigating effect of government measures. These substantial anti-crisis measures however worsened the state of public finances, as the deficit reached 9.3% of the GDP and the public debt 60% of GDP. In addition to this, inflation reached a peak of 7%, in April 2020, while the lari was depreciated by 14% against the United States Dollar (USD) in the same year. The crisis is further exacerbated by the large informal sector, the high share of vulnerable workers, high unemployment and low saving rates (OECD, 2020[6]).

Nonetheless, Georgia has been experiencing recovery throughout 2021. The GDP contraction persisted in the first quarter of 2021, which registered -4.5%, but the trend was reversed in the second quarter of the year. GDP growth is now expected to reach 7.7% in 2021, mainly due to a reprise in key sectors such as tourism, manufacturing, construction and services, as well as to an increase in remittances and exports, which have been faster than anticipated (German Economic Team, 2021[7]). Public deficit is expected to narrow to 6.5% of GDP, and public debt should decrease compared to the 2020 level (German Economic Team, 2021[7]). These improvements are expected to continue in the following years, as projections envisage the achievement of the 3% target for the fiscal deficit before 2025, as well as a continuous decline of public debt in the years to come (World Bank, 2021[8]). However, inflation has risen to 12.8% y-o-y in August 2021, due to an increase in utility and commodity prices as well as elevated input costs due to the currency depreciation (IMF, 2021[9]), but it is expected to diminish from the beginning of 2022 onwards (IMF, 2021[9]). The lari has indeed been stabilised throughout 2021, and it has slightly appreciated, 0.8%, in real effective terms (IMF, 2021[5]). The positive trend should continue, as current World Bank forecasts expect a GDP growth of around 6% in 2022 as well as in 2023 (World Bank, 2021[10]). The recovery however is highly dependent on the country capability to vaccinate its population, and hence to avoid new waves of infections, and on its capacity to maintain a stable political environment that will foster the necessary reforms.

Table 0.1. Key macroeconomic indicators for Georgia, 2015-2020

Indicator	Unit of Measurement	2015	2016	2017	2018	2019	2020	2021[2]	2022[2]
GDP Growth**	Percentage y-o-y	3	2.9	4.8	4.8	5	-6.2	7.7	5.8
Inflation**	Percentage average	4.0	2.1	6.0	2.6	4.8	5.2	13.1	3.2
Government balance[1]**	Percentage of GDP	-1.3	-1.6	-0.5	-0.9	-1.8	-9.3	-6.5	-3.6
Current account balance*	Percentage of GDP	-11.8	-12.5	-8.0	-6.8	-5.5	-12.4	-10.0	-7.6
Exports of goods and service*	Percentage of GDP	40.9	40.8	46.5	50.6	54.8	37.4	-	-
Imports of goods and services*	Percentage of GDP	57.9	56.0	57.5	61.2	63.8	55.9	-	-
FDI net inflows*	Percentage of GDP	11.6	11.0	11.8	7.2	7.7	-	-	-
General government gross debt**	Percentage of GDP	36.6	40.2	38.6	37.5	40.4	60.6	54.2	53.6
Domestic credit to private sector*	Percentage of GDP	51.0	58.7	58.1	62.6	67.7	-	-	-
Unemployment**	Percentage of total labour force	21.9	21.7	21.6	19.2	17.6	18.5	22.1	-
Nominal GDP**	USD billion	14.9	15.1	16.2	17.6	15.7	15.7	18.2	20.5

Note: [1] General government net lending/borrowing [2] Latest forecasts available
Source: * (World Bank, 2021[11]) and (World Bank, 2021[10]) ** (IMF, 2021[12]), (IMF, 2021[13]), and (IMF, 2021[14]).

SME sector

SMEs play a predominant role in the economy of Georgia, representing 99.7% of enterprises in 2019. Their economic contribution has been growing over the past years: in 2019, SMEs amounted for 65% of total employment and 59.3% of value added, up from 58.1% in 2015 (Figure 0.1). They are concentrated in Tbilisi, with the capital city representing 51% of SME employment and 63% of value added (Figure 0.2).

Figure 0.1. Value added by firm size, 2015-2019

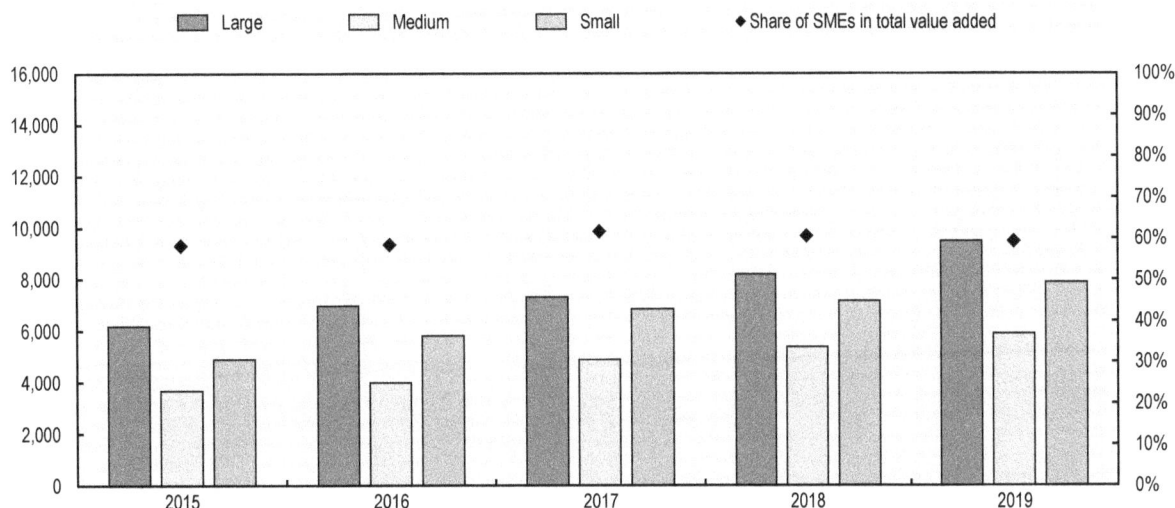

Source: Geostat.

Figure 0.2. Regional breakdown of firms

Percentage of total, 2019

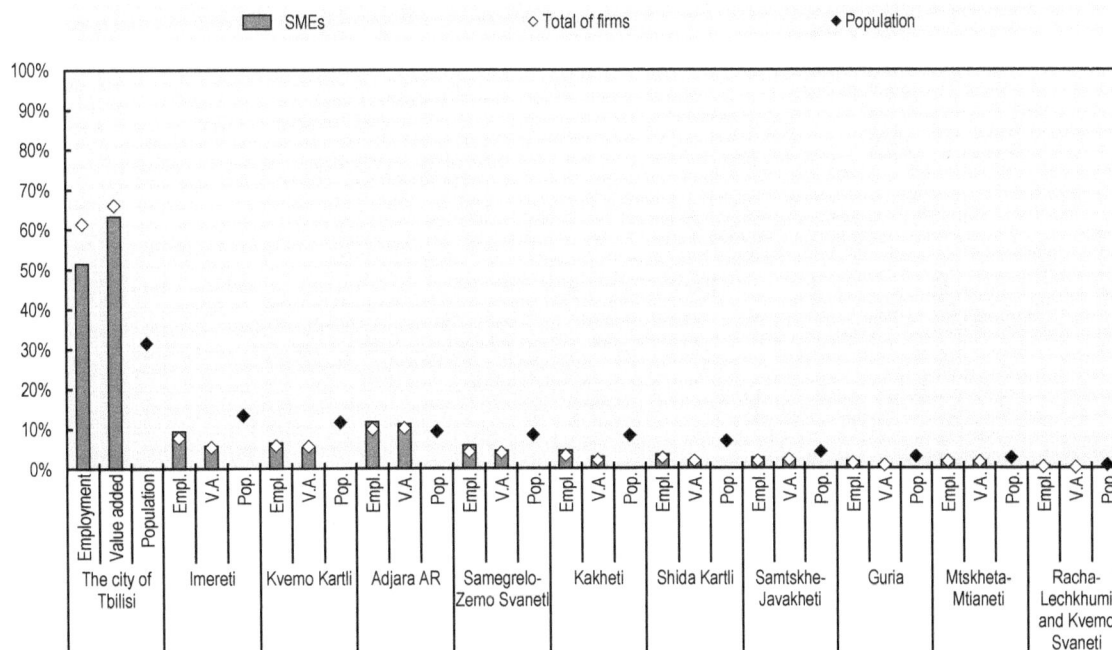

Note: Employment corresponds to the average annual number of persons employed. Data unavailable for Abkhazia.
Source: OECD analysis based on Geostat.

However, SMEs remain mostly concentrated in low-value-added sectors such as trade (including repair of vehicles), manufacturing and construction – these gathered 39% of Georgian SMEs in 2017.

The development of the SME sector in Georgia has been fostered by significant policy efforts provided by the Government. From an already strong position, Georgia has made further progress since 2016: its performance is reflected in the SME Policy Index (SMEPI) (OECD et al., 2020[1]), where the country appears as the best regional performer. It notably adopted a more strategic approach to small and medium-sized entrepreneurship development through targeted initiatives, including through the SME Development Strategy 2016-2020 and respective action plans, which have helped to improve the operational environment for SMEs drastically.

Box 0.1. SME Policy Index: Eastern Partner Countries 2020

The Small Business Act for Europe and the SME Policy Index

The SME Policy Index is a benchmarking tool for assessing and monitoring progress in the design and implementation of SME policies against EU and international best practice. Structured around the ten principles of the EU's Small Business Act for Europe (SBA), it was developed by the OECD, the EU, the European Bank for Reconstruction and Development, and the European Training Foundation to assess the business environment for SMEs and provide relevant recommendations to address remaining challenges.

The Index is structured around five thematic pillars, further broken down in 12 dimensions based on the ten SBA principles. A cross-cutting level playing field pillar was added to the third edition of the Index (published in 2020, following assessments in 2012 and 2016).

2020 findings for Georgia

Georgia has made significant progress since 2016, confirming itself as the top performer in the EaP region. Its efforts to implement previous OECD recommendations particularly stand out regarding entrepreneurial learning and women's entrepreneurship (+57% increase on average), and SME skills (+38%). The country's performance remains weak with regards to bankruptcy and second chance policies, as well as SME greening.

Figure 0.3. SME Policy Index scores for Georgia

Country scores by dimension, 2020 vs 2016

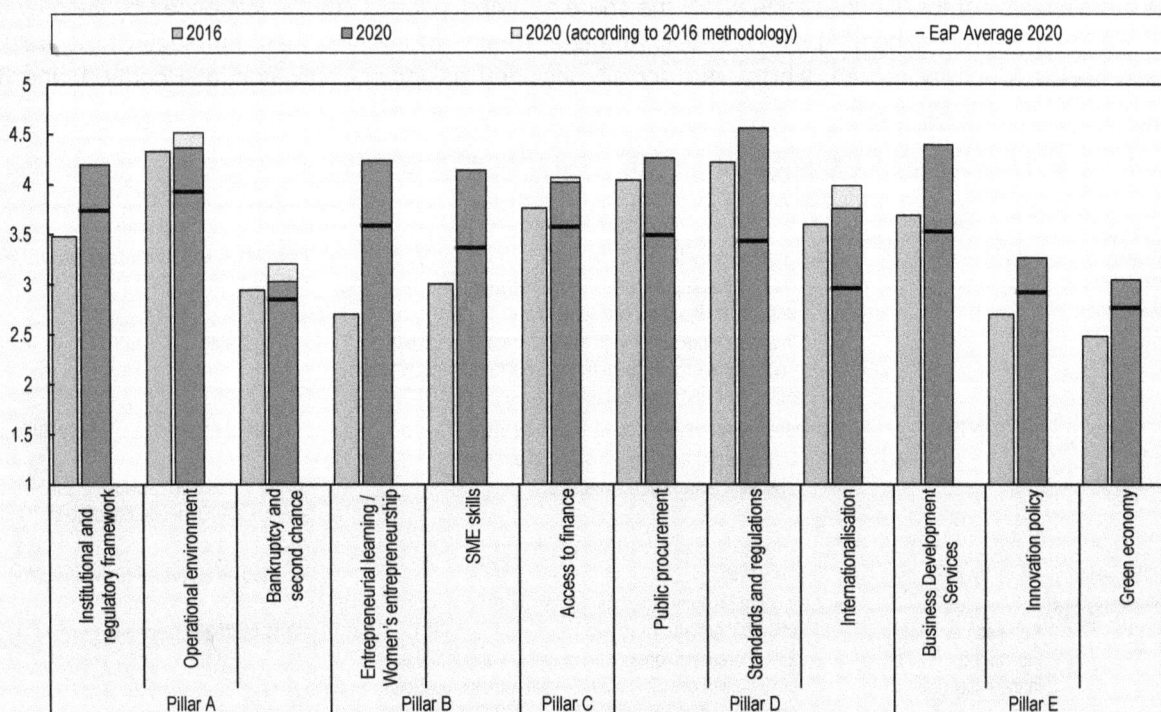

Source: (OECD et al., 2020[1]).

The previous SME strategy 2016-2020 entailed three overall targets – output growth, persons employed, and productivity growth. As illustrated below (Figure 0.4), the targets have been achieved very early in the implementation period of the Strategy, which provides evidence of the positive developments in the SME sector, but also that more ambitious targets could have been considered.

Figure 0.4. SME Development Strategy 2016-2020 overall targets

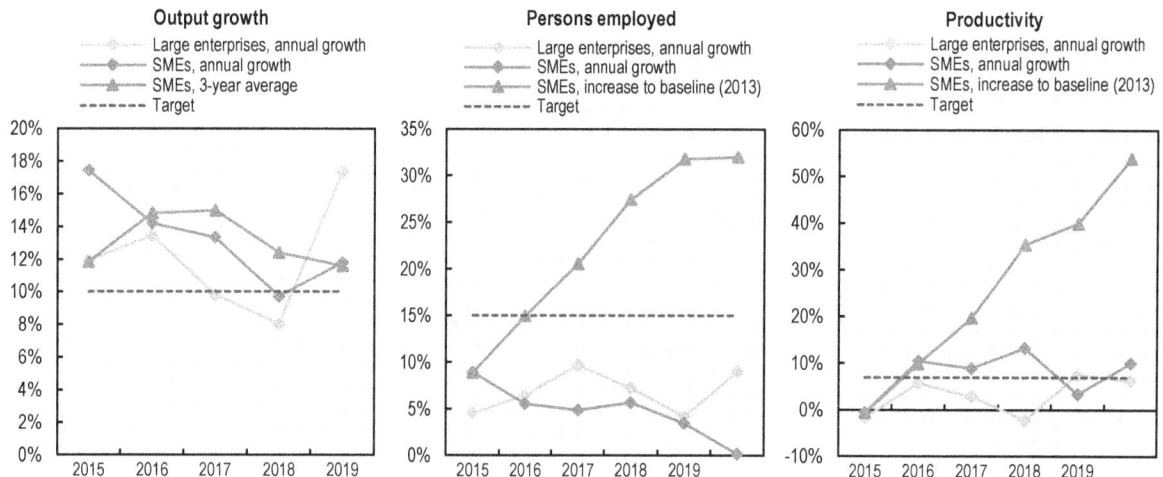

Source: Geostat.

The OECD has proposed some KPIs to monitor the impact of the new SME Strategy 2021-2025 (Table 0.2). While the first draft of the new Strategy planned to use the percentage of SMEs in total output as an overall target for the document, the OECD suggested to rather use SME output growth, and to use it as impact indicator for Priority 1 instead, for the share of SMEs in total output is influenced by the growth of large firms. As recommended by the OECD, the final version of the document foresees SMEs' value added and productivity growth, which were initially included as impact indicator for Priority 1 and 3, respectively, as overall targets.

Table 0.2. Overall targets suggested by the OECD for the new Strategy

Indicator	Initial draft	OECD suggestion	Final draft
Share of SMEs in total output	70% by 2025	SMEs **output growth**: +30% by 2025 • Use SMEs output growth instead of share, as the latter is affected by the growth of large firms • Indicator more suitable to monitor Priority 1, for better institutional environment helps firms to operate, which is reflected in increased activity (i.e. output)	Included as impact indicator for Priority 1 +20 by 2025
Number of SME employees	+15% by 2025	Number of **persons employed**: +15% by 2025 • Use persons employed instead of employees • The 15% target seems realistic	Number of employees +10% by 2025 (target decreased because of the sharp, COVID-induced decline in 2020)
SMEs' value added	+20% by 2025 Foreseen as impact indicator for Priority 1 in the initial draft	+30% by 2025 • It could be considered as overall impact indicator instead of output growth • 20% increase might not be ambitious enough given the 60% growth over 2015-2019 – but remains acceptable given uncertainties related to the COVID-19 impact	Included as an overall target indicator +20% by 2025 (in nominal terms)
SMEs' productivity	+20% by 2025 Foreseen as impact indicator for Priority 3 in the initial draft	+25% by 2025 • It could be considered as overall impact indicator, as SME productivity can be improved by all strategic priorities	Included as an overall target indicator +20% by 2025

With regard to the institutional framework, the main stakeholders in charge of SME policy implementation in Georgia are the Ministry of Economy and Sustainable Development (MoESD), and the two SME support agencies, Enterprise Georgia and Georgia's Innovation and Technology Agency (GITA), both created in 2014. Enterprise Georgia is responsible for the implementation of SME support programmes. It aims at improving private sector competitiveness by working on three main directions, i.e. business development, export promotion, and attraction of foreign direct investments. Its flagship programme, *Produce in Georgia*, includes financing tools such as co-financing of interest rate on commercial loans and matching grants. GITA complements this approach by focusing on support to start-ups, innovation and R&D, especially in the ICT field, through financing and non-financial instruments further detailed in this report. Other Ministries listed in Figure 0.5 are also closely involved, as well as the Business Ombudsman of Georgia and several legal entities under public law (LEPL), e.g. the national statistical agency Geostat, the National Competition Agency, GEOSTM, the Rural Development Agency, the National Tourism Administration, the Agency of Protected Areas, and the Service for Accounting, Reporting and Auditing Supervision (SARAS). The private sector is increasingly participating in policymaking and implementation via a number of business associations.

Figure 0.5. Institutional framework for SME policies in Georgia

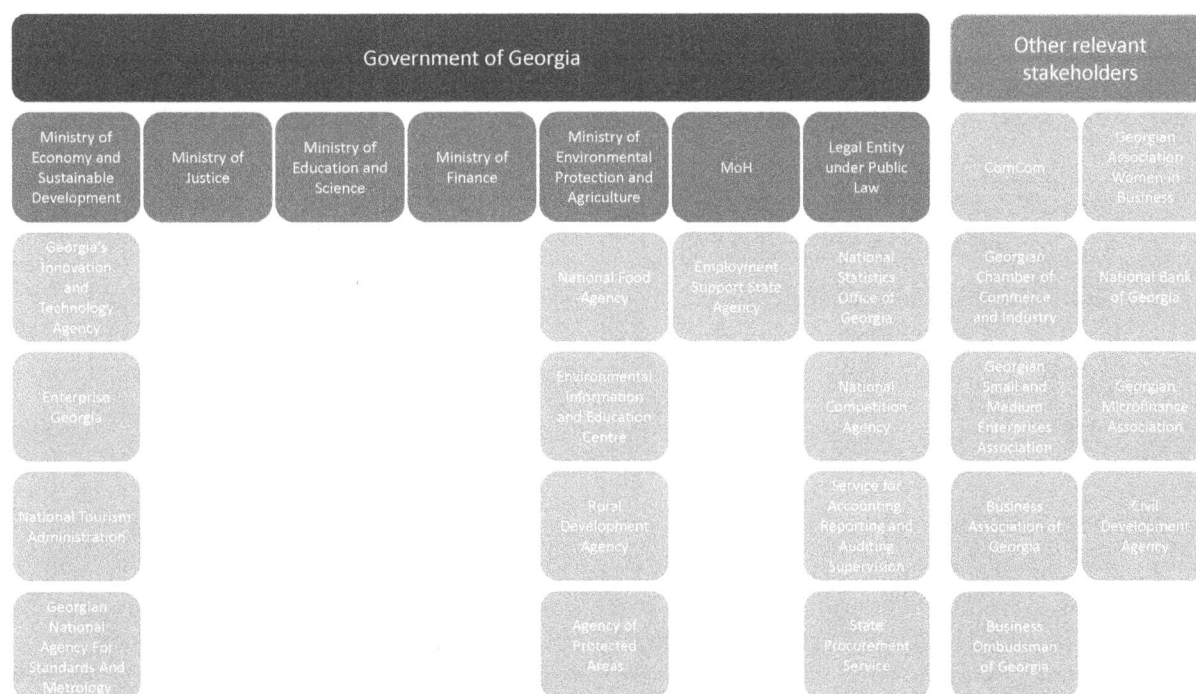

Note: MoH refers to the Ministry of Internally Displaced Persons from the Occupied Territories, Labour, Health, and Social Affairs of Georgia. ComCom refers to the Communication Commission (former GNCC – Georgian National Communications Commission).
Source: OECD authors based on fact-finding questionnaires, working group meetings and desk research.

COVID-19 impact on SMEs

As outlined above, the COVID-19 crisis has taken a toll on the economy. Georgian SMEs have been particularly affected by the crisis for several reasons. SMEs appear over-represented in sectors that were most affected by containment measures, such as services, tourism, and retail trade. In general, they are less capitalised than larger firms, which increases the risk of liquidity shortages, and they have fewer clients and suppliers, making them more vulnerable to supply chain disruption and loss of revenues. Finally, the fact that they are less digitalised than large firms (see Part 2) results in them being less able to transition to remote work. The strong economic impact of the crisis on SMEs has been highlighted by the World Bank Enterprise surveys carried out in June 2020 and October/November 2020 (Figure 0.6).

Figure 0.6. Impact of the COVID-19 crisis on Georgian SMEs

2020

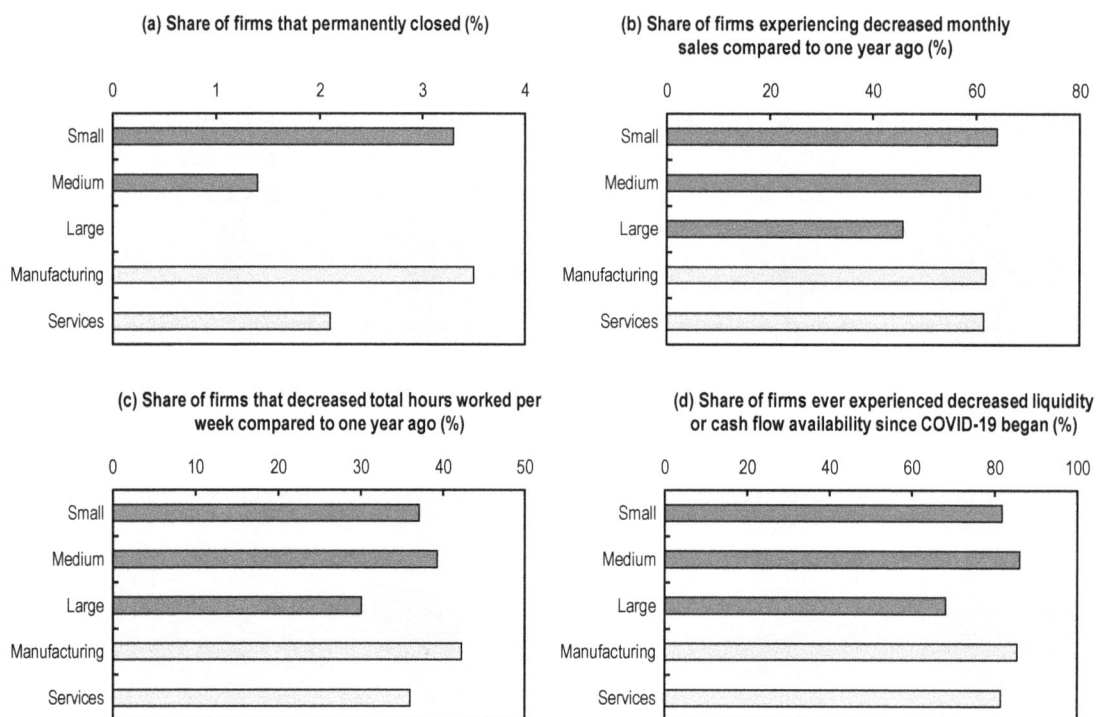

Note: Panel (a) refers to the percentage of firms confirmed permanently closed since the COVID-19 pandemic was declared. Value for large firms in Panel (a) is zero.
Source: (World Bank, 2020[15]).

However, the Government responded with one of the most generous anti-crisis support package of the EaP countries, including a range of tools dedicated to SMEs. It encompassed measures to support labour, such as income tax exemptions, unemployment benefits and one-off assistance of GEL 300 to the self-employed, as well as property tax deferrals, additional VAT refunds, utility subsidies, and credit repayment deferrals. Financial instruments were also implemented, such as the expansion of the credit guarantee scheme expected to benefit up to 1 000 SMEs, improved co-financing conditions (e.g. with an extension of the loan/leasing co-funding period), and interest subsidies for existing loans for some of the hardly hit sectors (more detail on page 35). The Government also adopted sector-specific plans for tourism, agriculture and construction. As of October/November 2020, almost half of Georgian SMEs had received government assistance – however, this share appears to be below that of large firms (75%) (World Bank, 2020[15]).

1 Recommendations for Georgia's SME development strategy 2021-2025

At the request of the Ministry of Economy and Sustainable Development of Georgia and with the support of the EU4Business Initiative, the OECD, in co-operation with GIZ, assisted the Georgian government in preparing a new SME Development Strategy 2021-2025 and a first related Action Plan. This chapter summarises the main issues identified by the OECD for each of the Strategy's seven dimensions, and recommends additional specific policy measures to be considered for future action plans. It also suggests key performance indicators to monitor progress in the strategy's implementation

Priority 1: Strengthening the institutional framework and operational environment for SMEs

State of play

Over the past five years, Georgia has considerably improved the institutional and operational environment for businesses with the implementation of its SME Development Strategy 2016-2020. SMEs now benefit from an improved institutional and regulatory framework, which is reflected in international assessments such as the OECD *SME Policy Index: Eastern Partner countries 2020* (the "SMEPI"), in which Georgia stands out as the best performer among EaP countries, including on the SMEPI's "Pillar A", which assesses the institutional, regulatory and operational environment (OECD et al., 2020[1]). Georgia also considerably expanded and formalised public-private participation in policymaking: several dedicated platforms have been set up, such as the Private Sector Development Advisory Council and the Consultation Council on Georgian Trade under the MoESD, which have helped to formalise public-private consultations and hold meetings more regularly. As a result, private sector participation has become more inclusive and comments provided by the private sector have increasingly been reflected in draft laws (Institute for Development of Freedom and Information, 2019[16]).

With regards to the operational environment, Georgia has significantly expanded the availability of e-government services. The single portal www.my.gov.ge, launched in 2012 and operated by a new Digital Governance Agency under the Ministry of Justice of Georgia since 2020 (previously by the Data Exchange Agency), appears as one of the most advanced one-stop solutions of the Eastern Partner region. Already offering close to 500 services to citizens and businesses in 2019, the platform was further developed in response to the COVID-19 pandemic and now provides about 700 online services in a wide range of areas. The number of users also increased (+40% in 2020), making this governmental website one of the most visited ones according to the UNDP (2021[17]).

In addition, the government significantly reformed the insolvency and rehabilitation system, for a long time considered as one of the biggest weaknesses in the country's business environment. A new insolvency law, "On Rehabilitation and Collective Satisfaction of Creditors", was adopted in September 2020 and entered into force on 1 April 2021. This reform notably promotes rehabilitation and job preservation over liquidation while also emphasising creditor protection (Government of Georgia, 2020[18]). To this end, it introduces new concepts such as regulated agreements, a facilitated procedure under which the debtor can negotiate debt restructuring with creditors to aim for the continuation of the company's activities. The law also empowers insolvency practitioners and increases the transparency of proceedings by introducing a dedicated electronic system through which applications can be filled, convocations to creditors' meetings, minutes and decisions can be quickly published and information exchanged. In this regard, the order of the Minister of Justice №696 „On the approval of the insolvency practitioner, the production of an unified registry of insolvency practitioners and the approval of the selection terms and conditions through the electronic system of insolvency practitioners", issued on 30 March 2021, defines the types and conditions for the authorisation of the insolvency practitioner, and rules for maintaining a unified registry of such practitioners. It also determines the main issues related to certification as well as the rules and conditions to appoint a practitioner as a rehabilitation/bankruptcy manager or rehabilitation/CVA supervisor through the electronic system.

The Government of Georgia also approved the "Law on Entrepreneurs", which came into force in 2021 and aims at improving the legal framework, regulating internal corporate relations and increasing transparency in this area while promoting entrepreneurial freedom. Additionally, the National Agency of Public Registry aims to create an electronic portal provided by the law to promote digitalisation.

Moreover, the Government of Georgia has taken several steps to facilitate SMEs' access to information on new laws and regulations. Regarding approximation with EU standards for instance, businesses can turn to information centres and to the dedicated web portal dcfta.gov.ge. Yet SMEs continue to report finding it difficult to stay up-to-date on regulatory changes and related opportunities, according to interviews with private sector associations.

In addition to strengthening its regulatory environment, Georgia has also achieved significant progress in developing regulatory impact assessment (RIA). RIA is a policy tool used to analyse the costs, benefits and effects of a new or existing regulation, allowing the government to evaluate their policies and adapt them if needed. It now has to be performed for a set of identified business-related draft laws introduced by the Government, and a dedicated methodology has been adopted early 2020 (Government of Georgia, 2020[19]). Nevertheless, the regulatory impact specifically on SMEs through an "SME test" is not systematically considered. Such an "SME test" evaluates the specific impact of regulations on SMEs through an *ex-ante* and *ex-post* analysis of the costs and benefits of the initiative, and involves SMEs and their representative organisations in the process.

Unsurprisingly, the economic crisis triggered by the pandemic has led to significant difficulties for companies, including an increase in business failures (see Figure 0.6 in the Introduction). Georgian SMEs have been particularly affected by containment measures, which caused a sharp drop of revenues and liquidity shortages: in October 2020, 82% and 86% of small and medium firms, respectively, reported having experienced decreased liquidity or cash flow availability since the pandemic began (against 68% of large firms) (World Bank, 2020[15]). Some 5.4% of small and 2% of medium businesses were confirmed or assumed permanently closed by October 2020 (0.4% of large ones), but this number is expected to rise as governmental support measures are gradually lifted.

Way forward

Promote restructuring and entrepreneurial fresh start

In light of the long-lasting COVID-19 crisis and the decrease of governmental emergency support measures, many companies are likely to encounter financial difficulties. SMEs are particularly vulnerable in that regard, given their limited financial reserves and free cash flow. The number of business failures is therefore expected to rise. In order to limit the spike bankruptcies and liquidations of financially distressed but otherwise viable companies, it is becoming increasingly important to help businesses detect bankruptcy warning signs, and to promote entrepreneurial rehabilitation. Georgia has, as recommended by the OECD, added an objective on promoting rehabilitation in the Strategy. In view of this goal, Georgia could consider the following measures:

- **Implement an early-warning system:** several types of early-warning mechanisms exist to help entrepreneurs understand the risk of insolvency and take action to avoid failure. These can be self-tests, training courses for entrepreneurs in need, and/or advisory services, such as Denmark's *EarlyWarning* programme (see Box 1.1).
- **Promote alternative dispute resolution mechanisms:** Insolvency proceedings can be quite costly and are rarely the most suitable option for SMEs suffering financial difficulties. Strengthening out-of-court procedures, such as arbitration and mediation, and prioritising them whenever possible, would offer entrepreneurs faster and cheaper ways to find common grounds with creditors and help them avoid selling their assets when fearing insolvency. The above-mentioned "regulated agreement" introduced by the new insolvency law is a welcome step in this regard, and should be used whenever possible.
- **Enact a strategy to promote second chance:** the recent improvements in the insolvency regime could be complemented by a dedicated second-chance policy, i.e. a policy to facilitate the rehabilitation of honest entrepreneurs who failed and enable them to make a fresh start. Such a strategy could be based on the possibility of being discharged from debt after a set period, to remove discriminatory provisions such as stricter rules on access to finance, and offer support

services for a fresh start (e.g. training and mentoring, as done by the DanubeChance2.0 project (Box 1.1)).

Box 1.1. Good practice examples on early warning and second chance

Early Warning Denmark (EAD)

Launched in 2007, *Early Warning Denmark* is a national programme offering free, impartial and confidential advice to SMEs in financial distress and at risk of insolvency. Bringing together about 100 volunteering advisors (experienced managers, business owners and specialists), 15-20 insolvency lawyers and 8 early warning consultants, EAD unfolds in three steps after receiving a company request:

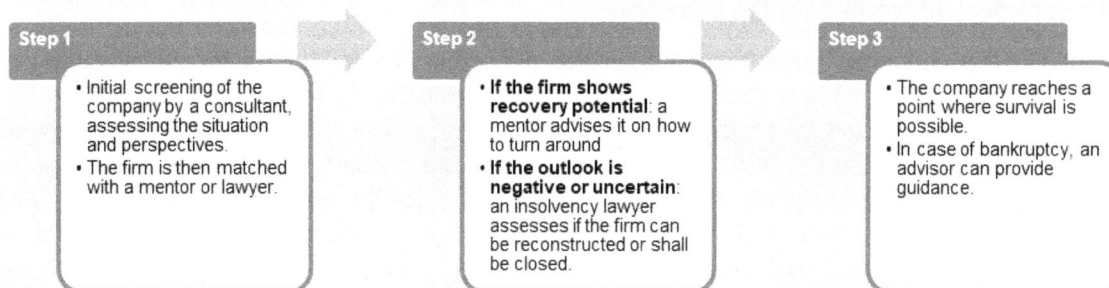

Step 1	Step 2	Step 3
• Initial screening of the company by a consultant, assessing the situation and perspectives. • The firm is then matched with a mentor or lawyer.	• **If the firm shows recovery potential**: a mentor advises it on how to turn around • **If the outlook is negative or uncertain**: an insolvency lawyer assesses if the firm can be reconstructed or shall be closed.	• The company reaches a point where survival is possible. • In case of bankruptcy, an advisor can provide guidance.

Evaluation studies have highlighted the programme's efficiency, showing that surviving companies that participated in it have maintained or improved their performance indicators. As for those that declared bankrupt, they did so with a lower debt to the public sector than firms that had not participated in the programme. Over 5 500 SMEs have taken part in the programme since its beginning, half of which managed to survive. As many companies decide to ask for these services once the situation is already critical, EAD is currently considering ways to engage with companies at an earlier stage.

DanubeChance2.0

This multi-year project was launched in 2018 to foster second-chance entrepreneurship in the Danube area (Austria, Bosnia and Herzegovina, Bulgaria, Czech Republic, Croatia, Germany, Hungary, Moldova, Romania, Serbia, Slovakia, Slovenia, and Ukraine). Its comprehensive approach consists of business acceleration and re-structuring services such as a self-assessment methodology, trainings and mentoring. It builds on partnerships with public and private stakeholders (tech parks, ministries, entrepreneurship centres, research centres, SME agencies, business networks).

Sources: (Early Warning Europe, 2021[20]) and (Danube Transnational Programme, 2021[21]).

Apply an SME test in the process of adopting new regulations

Compliance costs of regulation are often disproportionately high for SMEs. RIA can help estimate these costs, and identify potentially less costly solutions and/or mitigating measures. Georgia could consider applying SME-specific RIA systematically with the introduction of an "SME test", for which the European Commission's "Better Regulation Toolbox" offers practical guidance (European Commission, 2017[22]). This approach should be accompanied by public-private consultations to discuss the results and identify opportunities to lower compliance costs for small firms.

Step up awareness-raising initiatives on changing regulations for SMEs

In addition to the above-mentioned DCFTA information centres, where SMEs can find information regarding the reforms and legislative initiatives within the framework of the Free Trade agreement with the EU, the government could develop more initiatives to raise SMEs' awareness of new laws and regulations. As recommended by the OECD, Georgia added a dedicated objective to the Strategy on the strengthening of the public-private dialogue. Other measures could be considered, e.g. events, social media campaigns, television advertising and print information campaigns.

Conduct impact evaluation of government-sponsored support programmes

The Strategy envisages a strengthening of existing government programmes to support SMEs and the development of new ones. To this end, financial resources for flagship government programmes and implementing agencies are expected to increase substantially every year until 2025 (+29% for Enterprise Georgia's *Produce in Georgia* and +421% for GITA by 2025) (Government of Georgia, 2021[23]). It is therefore increasingly important to monitor these programmes and their impact, to ensure that they achieve their policy objectives. Enterprise Georgia has started working in that direction: within GIZ's project Clusters4Development, the agency is currently developing an impact assessment framework to be piloted at the end of 2021. To this end, Syspons GmbH, its German partner, has conducted a Monitoring and evaluation capacity assessment of the agency and helped identify relevant impact indicators, which will be disaggregated notably by firm size and gender. Building on this, a good practice in terms of methodology would be to use econometric estimations of the "treatment effect", i.e. make comparison between samples of SMEs who received and did not receive support. Surveys of beneficiaries and consultations with stakeholders can also provide qualitative feedback.

Broaden statistics on SMEs

The production of quality statistics is essential to evidence-based policymaking. The national Statistics Office of Georgia (Geostat) has made significant progress over the past years in producing and disseminating statistics on SMEs: it revised the SME definition to include number of employees as well as company turnover, making the definition compliant to EU standards and the data internationally comparable. It also started performing regular surveys to monitor a variety of aspects such as number of employees, wages, ownership by gender and business location, and publishes since 2018 data on exports by business size. However, size-disaggregated data remain unavailable for some critical areas, such as digitalisation, gender, and SME financing. As the government intends to undertake substantial work on these topics, the Strategy could treat these areas as priority directions for the expansion of size-disaggregated statistics. International databases can serve as examples, such as the OECD *ICT Access and Usage by Businesses Database* for indicators on SME digitalisation and the OECD *Scoreboard on Financing SMEs* for access to finance.

Table 1.1. Overview of recommendations to strengthen the institutional and operational environment

Recommendation	Status	Details
Promote restructuring and entrepreneurial fresh start	◑	An objective dedicated to *developing the bankruptcy and rehabilitation system* was added to the Strategy. It foresees further legislative changes and measures to foster rehabilitation.
		In addition, Georgia should consider introducing an early-warning system and initiatives to promote second chance. These initiatives could start as small-scale pilots.
Apply an SME test in the process of adopting new regulations	●	The Strategy foresees the application of the SME test to legislative changes. Its effective implementation should be ensured, and public-private consultations to discuss the results considered.
Step up awareness-raising initiatives on changing regulations for SMEs	◑	An objective dedicated to *developing public-private dialogue* (PPD) *and awareness-raising for SMEs on changing regulations* was added to the Strategy. It includes additional awareness-raising activities and the strengthening of public-private dialogue platforms.
		However, the impact of these activities could be better monitored, e.g. by tracking the share of comments to government strategies, action plans, laws and regulations received during PPDs that have been reflected in the final versions by the Government.
Conduct impact evaluation of government-sponsored support programmes	●	A provision was added to the Strategy to introduce an impact assessment framework for some state-sponsored programmes, which should be conducted for four programmes by 2025.
Broaden statistics on SMEs	◑	The Strategy includes an objective on improving SME statistics, and precisions were added to the logical framework to specify the new areas covered, which include gender.
		Moving forward, Georgia could consider producing statistics on SME digitalisation and financing.

○ Not incorporated   ◑ Partly incorporated   ● Incorporated

Table 1.2. Suggested KPIs to monitor the improvement of the institutional and operational environment

KPI	Description/rationale	Baseline (2019)	Target (2025)	Source of data
SMEs output growth	This indicator was initially planned as an overall target for the whole Strategy, but it appears more suitable for Priority 1: a better institutional environment helps firms to operate, and can thereby increase activity (i.e. output).	GEL 27.7 bln	20% increase	Geostat
OECD SME Policy Index score for "Institutional and regulatory framework"	This SMEPI indicator includes institutional framework, RIA and PPD, and is thereby closely related to this priority.	4.20	Improved score	OECD SME Policy Index
Impact assessment performed for selected state support programmes	This indicator goes in line with the OECD recommendation to evaluate both existing and new SME support programmes.	1 programme	4 programmes	LEPL Enterprise Georgia's report
% of trained staff reporting that they will use the skills learned at the training in their daily work	This is an outcome indicator, suggested to replace "% of trained staff", which was rather an output indicator. To obtain the data, a simple survey among training participants could be done some time after the training, e.g. an email sent to them 3 - 6 months later	n/a	70%	Progress report of SME Action Plan (AP)
Change in the number of business entities operating in the relevant market following decisions by the Competition Agency	This is an outcome indicator, suggested to replace "number of investigations conducted", which was rather an output indicator.	n/a	Positive change	Annual report of Georgian National Competition Agency
Increase in the number of jobs in the relevant market following decisions by the Competition Agency	This is an outcome indicator, suggested to replace "number of recommendations issued by the Competition Agency", which was rather an output indicator.	n/a	Positive change	Annual Report of Georgian National Competition Agency

KPI	Description/rationale	Baseline (2019)	Target (2025)	Source of data
% of users who find e-government services 1) useful and 2) easy to use	This outcome indicator can help assess the quality of services. It could be automated e.g. by a screen with 2 simple questions appearing on the page when the user has finished using the service, i.e. before logging out.	n/a	80%	My.gov.ge
% of insolvency procedures which resulted in rehabilitation rather than liquidation of the enterprise	This outcome indicator can help assess the effectiveness of the new Insolvency law.	5%	No less than 15% in total	Report of the Ministry of Justice of Georgia

Note: This table only includes the KPIs that have been added to the Priority upon OECD recommendation. It does not reflect exhaustively the comments provided by the OECD, e.g. on improving KPIs that were already included in the initial draft of the logical framework. Baseline and target values are those included in the adopted version of the logical framework.

Priority 2: Fostering the development of entrepreneurial skills and raising the entrepreneurial culture of SMEs

State of play

Georgia has achieved important improvements in human capital development since 2016, making it the top performer among EaP countries on the *SME skills* dimension in the OECD SMEPI 2020 (OECD et al., 2020[1]). In particular, entrepreneurial learning has been given greater importance in the Georgian education system, notably through the "Unified Strategy for Education and Science 2017-2021" and related action plans (Ministry of Education and Science of Georgia, 2017[24]). Entrepreneurship is now considered as a key competence and has been introduced in national school curricula at all levels of education.

Moreover, entrepreneurship and skills development has been fostered by the introduction of several non-formal learning initiatives. For example, GITA has launched FabLabs (Fabrication Laboratories), where people can access tools and knowledge to develop and test their projects, including start-up ideas. 22 of them have been established across the country as of early 2021, covering 12 cities in nine regions (FabLab Georgia, 2021[25]).

The creation of a labour market information system (LMIS hereafter – lmis.gov.ge) constituted an important achievement of the previous SME Strategy. Established in 2016, it addresses labour market information shortfalls by providing regularly updated data on market trends, e.g. employment, demand for workforce, wages, investments, and education (including vocational education).

Yet, despite important progress, indicators suggest that there is a persistent need for skills development in the country. Graduates' skills do not always correspond to employers' expectations. SMEs continue to cite this skills mismatch as one of the main problems they face (Figure 1.1), and employers cite the lack of required qualifications as the main obstacle to filling announced vacancies (Labour Market Information System, 2020[26]). Georgia's scores in international rankings on the skillset of graduates and ease of finding skilled employees also remain low (ranked 125th and 120th out of 141, respectively, in the *Global Competitiveness Report 2019* (World Economic Forum[27])).

Figure 1.1. Main obstacles encountered by SMEs

Percent of SMEs identifying the problem as a main obstacle, 2019

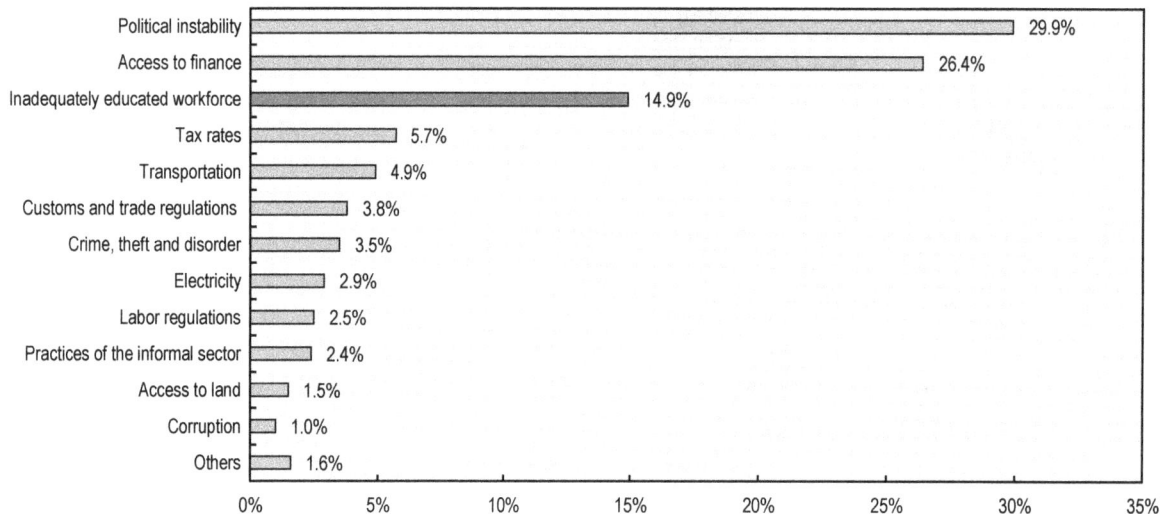

Source: (World Bank, 2019[28]).

Moreover, although several steps have been taken towards the development of vocational education and training (VET), recent LMIS surveys reveal that only 15% of enterprises in Georgia have employees with VET backgrounds (Labour Market Information System, 2020[26]). The co-operation between enterprises and VET institutions is still in its infancy, with only 2% of enterprises co-operating with VET schools, although 10% declared their need and/or wish to do so in the near future, e.g. through internships or work-based learning.

Finally, the effects of the COVID-19 pandemic on the education system and on the labour market call for additional measures to ensure the continuity of trainings and help workers adapt to labour demand. Containment and social distancing have increased the need for online training (OECD, 2020[29]), which would also help reaching remote areas, and the pandemic has highlighted the importance of digital skills, an area where there is still ample room for improvement. Georgia ranks 125th out of 141 in the (World Economic Forum, 2019[27]) *Global Competitiveness Report* (see also the dedicated figure in 2). In addition, economic lay-offs are on the rise as a result of the crisis; unemployment was up 24% in Q2 2021 y-o-y. It is therefore essential to facilitate the reallocation of affected workers across sectors and occupations (OECD, 2021[30]).

Way forward

Use re-skilling programmes to help laid-off workers transition to new jobs

The final version of the Strategy outlines the severe impact of the COVID-19 crisis on the economy, but it could be complemented by additional measures to tackle this. Some sectors, such as retail, catering and tourism, have been particularly affected by the crisis, and others like manufacturing, construction, and wholesale trade are at high risk (Human Rights Education and Monitoring Center, 2020[31]). While the job losses will continue to rise in these sectors, others such as technology, especially online platforms, and care services have increased workforce needs (European Training Foundation, 2021[32]) (OECD, 2021[30]). Although some of the effects of the COVID-19 pandemic on the job market are temporary, as they are associated with government restrictions, some changes caused by the crisis, such as the shift towards an increased use of technology, will have long-term consequences. Policies supporting the matching of workers with employers' needs, and thereby facilitating labour reallocation towards in-demand and more productive sectors, will therefore be critical for an effective recovery. Several tools can foster the re-skilling of laid-off workers, and could constitute interesting policy options: beyond the provision of trainings, developing skills assessment tools would enable individuals to better identify their crosscutting competencies and guide them to new job ideas, thereby facilitating their transition. Australia's Skills Match tool offers an interesting example in that regard: it allows job seekers to enter their working experience and skills and receive information on jobs that require their professional knowledge and abilities. In addition, the platform offers informative material on careers, labour market trends and employment projections, together with links to a number of relevant websites (JobOutlook, 2021[33]).

Strengthen industry/VET schools linkages

As outlined above, skills mismatch appears to be a persistent issue, while the LMIS survey highlighted the substantial unmet demand for VET students among enterprises. Incentivising companies, and notably SMEs, to co-operate with VET schools could help address this mismatch. This could be achieved by increasing opportunities for internships, apprenticeships, and work-based learning through both financial and non-financial measures – e.g. tax breaks, partial wage subsidies, formal partnerships between schools and firms, and/or SME involvement in the design of training.

Foster the development of online-based solutions for VET modules

The COVID-19 pandemic highlighted the need for online solutions for VET modules to help meet the increased demand for distance learning. In addition to providing online trainings, Georgia could consider developing teachers' digital skills, and creating a dedicated platform for all stakeholders (VET teachers, employers, learners) to share information and resources. Croatia, for instance, has set up a portal (http://nastava.asoo.hr) where stakeholders from various sectors can upload VET material (European Commission, 2020[34]). Users can thereby access trainings easily and free-of-charge, and the content published can serve as an example to develop additional modules.

Adopt a comprehensive approach to develop digital skills

Digital skills are increasingly in demand in the labour market, being now required for most occupations (OECD, 2021[30]). They are particularly important for SMEs in order to reap the benefits of digital technologies (e.g. reaching new clients through e-commerce, improving manufacturing with digital tools, developing customer insight through data analytics, etc.) and adapt to increasingly digitalised economies and societies. They can be classified in four categories, which can allow policymakers to understand which types of skills help people get the most out of digital technologies:

- **Foundation skills**, e.g. literacy and numeracy: these enable individuals to develop and acquire higher order cognitive skills needed in digital economies and societies, and help them adapt to an environment of fast and ever-changing technologies and labour market requirements. These are usually acquired in the formal education system;
- **Generic digital skills**, e.g. accessing information online and using software, which can be useful for all workers. On-the-job training on these can be very useful, especially for low-skilled workers;
- **Advanced digital skills**, e.g. skills needed to develop IT products and services such as programming, developing applications, managing networks), acquired by digital specialists;
- **Complementary skills**, e.g. cognitive skills, interpersonal skills (information processing, self-direction, problem solving, communication), managerial and organisational skills, allow to work in a digitalised environment.

While the Strategy plans to expand digital skills trainings, Georgia could step up its efforts in this field by adopting a comprehensive approach to digital literacy, building on the numerous policy options – e.g. needs assessment, trainings, resources, and multi-stakeholder initiatives[1].

---

[1] See Box 1.2 and the dedicated section in 2, which provides a detailed assessment of the state of digital skills in Georgia, the related policies implemented, as well as several policy options to foster their development

Box 1.2. Building a multifaceted approach to digital skills

Assessing SME needs

Self-diagnosis tools can be very useful to help SMEs identify their needs. The *Chambre des Métiers* of Luxembourg for instance has introduced Digicheck, an online self-assessment covering six topics – communication, management, human resources, security, regulation, and production and services. After a 10-15 minutes questionnaire, the tool generates a digital maturity profile and recommendations. The respondent can also consult an expert to discuss results. Such tools also enable the collection of anonymous data on digital skills gap.

Creating dedicated tools

Trainings: e.g. on how to digitalise processes, digital marketing/use of social networks, cybersecurity.

Handbooks: providing free and easily accessible guides – Singapore's Infocomm Media Development Agency offers sector-specific handbooks for SMEs (the *Industry Digital Plans*).

Single portal: creating a single information portal, such as Spain's Acelera PYME, can help raise SMEs' awareness of available services and extend the reach to regions.

Fostering multi-stakeholder initiatives

Official accreditation of competencies: setting a common reference framework for ICT knowledge enables to set standards, ensure the quality of programmes and learning outcomes, and ease the recruitment processes. The EU e-competence framework, built for SMEs in all industry sectors and encompassing 40 e-competences with 5 proficiency levels, is a good example in this regard.

Awareness-raising/peer-learning activities: dedicated events can also increase SMEs' awareness of the topic and resources available, and of the ways to introduce digital tools. The Federation of Finnish Enterprises organises free annual events all over the country, with conferences and peer-learning activities, and targeted at entrepreneurs at the early-stages of their digital transformation.

Source: (Digital Luxembourg[35]), (Infocomm Media Development Authority[36]), (Acelera PYMA[37]), (Small Business Standards, 2018[38]) and (Yrittajat, 2021[39]).

Table 1.3. Overview of recommendations to foster entrepreneurial skills development

Recommendation	Status	Details
Use re-skilling programmes to help laid-off workers transition to new jobs	○	The Strategy does not entail measures on re-skilling.
Strengthen industry/VET schools linkages	◑	A specific reference to increasing the cooperation between VET schools and SMEs was added to the Strategy, accompanied by an indicator on the number of work-based learning programmes. Additional measures could be considered in the future, as outlined above.
Foster the development of online-based solutions for VET modules	○	Some VET modules had been moved online in 2020, following the COVID-19 outbreak. Further online-based VET solutions are currently not defined as a priority for the MoESD.
Adopt a comprehensive approach to develop digital skills	◑	An objective on developing digital literacy was added, referring to the LogIn Georgia project (see Part 2), as well as an indicator on participants to digital skills trainings, which is expected to rise. Additional measures could be considered to foster SME digitalisation, as outlined in Box 1.2 and in Part 2.

○ Not incorporated   ◑ Partly incorporated   ● Incorporated

Table 1.4. Suggested KPIs to monitor skills development policies

KPI	Description/rationale	Baseline (2019)	Target (2025)	Source of data
% of training participants reporting that the skills learned at the training will help them to improve occupational safety in their business or to improve compliance with safety regulations	This is an outcome indicator, suggested to complement "number of trainings held", which was rather an output indicator. To obtain the data, a simple survey among training participants could be done some time after the training, e.g. an email sent to them 3 - 6 months later	0	80%	Report of LEPL Labour Inspection Service
% of trained entrepreneurs that think the skills and knowledge received during the training will be useful in improving/starting their own business	This is an outcome indicator, suggested to replace "number of trained entrepreneurs", which was rather an output indicator. To obtain the data, a simple survey among training participants could be done some time after the training, e.g. an email sent to them 3 - 6 months later	n/a	65%	Report of LEPL Enterprise Georgia LEPL Innovation and Technology Agency Georgian Chamber of Commerce and Industry (GCCI)
Number of graduates from short-term vocational training-retraining programmes	This is an outcome indicator, suggested to replace "number of newly enrolled students", which was rather an output indicator.	444 students annually	1 500 students annually	Report of the Ministry of Education and Science of Georgia
Number of introduced professional programmes with dual approach	This indicator was added by the MoESD upon OECD suggestion to add an indicator specific to work-based learning.	Up to 35	Up to 45	Report of the Ministry of Education and Science of Georgia
Number of LMIS users that find a job	This is an outcome indicator, suggested to replace "number of LMIS users", which was rather an output indicator. It can help assess the services' effectiveness.	908 persons, including 699 women	10% increase	Report of MoH
Number of trained companies reporting that the skills learned at the training will be helpful to implement Responsible Business Conduct/Environmental, Social and corporate Governance principles in their operations	The OECD initially suggested to use the "number of participating companies that have implemented RBC/ESG principles in their operations" as outcome indicator, but given that companies are not obliged to implement them, the MoESD opted for this other indicator.	n/a	70%	Reports of LEPL Enterprise Georgia

Note: This table only includes the KPIs that have been added to the Priority upon OECD recommendation. It does not reflect exhaustively the comments provided by the OECD, e.g. on improving KPIs that were already included in the initial draft of the logical framework. Baseline and target values are those included in the adopted version of the logical framework.

Priority 3: Improving access to finance

State of play

Over the implementation period of the previous SME Strategy, access to finance for SMEs became easier. Overall credit conditions for small firms improved: the average interest rates on loans to SMEs have decreased, more sharply for loans in foreign currency than for those in national currency, and the spread between interest rates on loans issued to SMEs and those provided to large firms has been reduced. The SME loan portfolio of commercial banks has been growing, showing a compound annual growth rate of 21.4% between 2015 and 2019 (National Bank of Georgia, 2019[40]).

In addition, the government has started developing a market of different alternative bank financing instruments. It introduced measures to develop microfinance and to support the uptake of new financing instruments, notably through regulations and training on fundraising for start-ups. A new Law on Investment Funds adopted in 2020 defines a legal framework for collective investment schemes and defines the different types of investment funds (Government of Georgia, 2020[41]). However, the potential of alternative finance remains largely untapped, and additional instruments could be promoted, in order to match the different needs and priorities of businesses. Leasing and factoring for instance are not yet widespread practices, and VC and business angel activity remain at a nascent phase. Digitalisation also offers new financing solutions that could provide SMEs with alternatives to bank financing, e.g. peer-to-peer and platform-based lending, which could support projects that traditional banks usually deem too small or too risky.

Several initiatives to foster financial literacy have been implemented. Georgia adopted a National Strategy for Financial Literacy after conducting an assessment of the population's financial literacy levels in 2016. The National Bank of Georgia (NBG) offers a financial education programme for micro and small enterprises, reaching a reported 1 200 beneficiaries in 2019. The NBG is also preparing brochures and trainings for entrepreneurs in agriculture, and financial literacy is taught in all Georgian schools since 2019 (National Bank of Georgia, 2019[40]).

Following the outbreak of the COVID-19 crisis, the government quickly introduced a wide range of financial instruments to support firms and counter liquidity shortages ensuing from the lockdowns and generalised slowdown of economic activity. Enterprise Georgia's credit guarantee scheme was increased to GEL 330 mln (USD 107 mln) in 2020, thereby securing a credit portfolio of GEL 2 bln in total with a 90% guarantee on new loans and 30% on restructuring. Firms also benefitted from improved co-financing conditions, e.g. with an extension of the loan/leasing co-funding period up to 36 months (from the previous 24). Some sectors that had been particularly affected were provided additional help, such as small hotels, restaurants, kindergartens and fitness facilities, which received 70-80% interest subsidies for existing loans, depending on the currency of the loan.

Despite these important measures, access to finance has remained one of the biggest long-term obstacles for SMEs, as outlined in the 2019 Enterprise Surveys (Figure 1.1). SMEs still face more difficulties to access financing than large firms: 20.6% of small firms are faced with rejection when applying for a loan, which is the case for only 2.6% of large firms. Yet the gap between them could be further reduced. Moreover, the importance of this issue is reflected in other dimensions of the Strategy, such as internationalisation, innovation, women entrepreneurship and the green economy (see relevant sections below).

Finally, while the Strategy acknowledges the impact of COVID-19 on businesses, further steps should be taken to prepare for the post-COVID era. As financial support measures are gradually phased out, firms risk moving from a liquidity to a solvency crisis: while the unprecedented amounts of governmental support have enabled many firms to weather the crisis during lockdowns, entrepreneurs are now highly likely to be faced with excessive debt levels, which calls for adapted public policy measures. Exit-from-lockdown policies should be based on several principles – promoting reopening and jobs, balancing protection and reallocation, and preventing avoidable bankruptcies (Blanchard, Philippon and Pisani-Ferry, 2020[42]). As the generosity of support measures is being gradually reduced as economies are reopening, measures for workers and firms should continue, but with some adjustments: while employment support should focus on the sectors that have been most affected by the crisis, loan guarantees should still be granted to viable and solvent firms. However, viable but insolvent firms should rather be incentivised to work out restructuring plans.

Way forward

Adapt COVID-19-related financial support packages to the post-crisis period

In light of the risk of a solvency crisis highlighted above, policymakers could:

- **Consider converting state-guaranteed loans into quasi equity instruments** in return for higher corporate income taxes to be paid for a given period in the future. This would lower debt liabilities on firms' balance sheets and increase the equity buffer, while improving their viability as operating businesses and ultimately lowering the risk of insolvency. This option might be preferable for small firms compared to proper equity as it requires less monitoring and avoids overburdening the state with small equity claims.

- **Target sectors that have been hit hardest and/or slowest to re-open:** as governments gradually reduce the overall support provided to firms and workers, they should try to maintain some support for sectors that have been most affected, such as services and tourism and might need more help and time to recover.

Strengthen the legal environment for alternative and digital financing instruments

Further steps could be taken to foster the development and uptake of a wider range of financing instruments, such as online-based lending, fintech and crowdfunding. Setting up a strong legal framework for alternative and digital finance solutions could help foster the emergence and growth of these practices. In that regard, Georgia could consider introducing regulatory sandboxes (EU4Digital, 2020[43]) (Attrey, Lesher and Lomax, 2020[44]) (Box 1.3). They are an effective tool to foster innovation in fintech and inform regulatory practice, building on the NBG's draft regulation on *Establishing Regulatory Laboratory (Sandbox) Framework*, for instance to introduce equity-based crowdfunding.

Box 1.3. Regulatory Sandboxes

Regulatory sandboxes are defined as concrete frameworks that provide a structured experimental context, ensuring a safe environment to test innovative technologies, products, services or approaches. In particular, they provide a waiving legal space that is structured on a case-by-case basis, which allows for the necessary flexibility. They serve as a foundation for informed regulatory design since they enable to collect evidence-based knowledge that informs regulators on the effects of the innovative tools, and guides the design of an appropriate regulatory framework.

The Abu Dhabi Global Market's Digital Sandbox

Supported by the Financial Services Regulatory Authority, the programme allows to experiment financial and digital products as well as services, with the aim of fostering the financial inclusion of marginalised populations in the Middle East and North Africa (MENA) region. The sandbox has enabled the testing of a variety of innovations, including Application Programme Interfaces (API), which allows for computers interconnection while easing user experience. This technology is also at the basis of a partnership with the ASEAN Financial Innovation Network that will ultimately allow sandbox participants to access the opportunities offered by international markets.

Innovation Link in the United Kingdom

It aims at innovating energy markets by enabling the trial of innovative business products, services, and models that do not fall within existing regulations. It assesses the necessity and provides entrepreneurs with advice on how to implement new tools under existing regulations. A sandbox solution was needed in only three cases, e.g. a waiver to test a new tariff based on smart home technology.

Sandbox Notification in Thailand

This sandbox targets innovation in the ICT sector to promote the adoption of 5G. It allows carrying out testing on different frequencies in a number of regions that are outside the existing regulations. The access to the use of the sandboxes is open to any other interested party that would like to apply 5G technology in their domain, in order to incentivise experimentation.

Source: (Council of the European Union, 2020[45]) and (Attrey, Lesher and Lomax, 2020[44]).

Further develop venture capital and business angels ecosystem

In line with OECD recommendations, an objective dedicated to further developing the VC and business angels ecosystem was added to the Strategy. This could be achieved by aligning the Law on Investment Funds with advanced EU VC regulations and by introducing additional legal provisions, such as a legal definition of business angel. Co-investment schemes and capacity building for VC managers could also be considered. A 2020 report by (EU4Digital, 2020[43]) provides a detailed analysis and recommendations on these topics.

Broaden financial education initiatives

Finally, to complement the financial education initiatives foreseen, additional measures could be considered to improve the evidence base on the financial literacy levels of entrepreneurs. The OECD International Network on Financial Education (INFE), a project gathering public institutions from over 125 countries, recently developed a dedicated survey to measure SMEs' financial literacy, which could serve as a useful reference for data collection and monitoring (OECD, 2020[46]).

Table 1.5. Overview of recommendations to improve SMEs' access to finance

Recommendation	Status	Details
Adapt COVID-19-related financial support packages to the post-crisis period	○	The Strategy does not refer to specific measures on adapting COVID-related financial support programmes. The recommendation should still be considered to tackle the effects of the crisis while ensuring fiscal sustainability in the long run.
Strengthen the legal environment for alternative and digital financing instruments	◑	The government has reported having reflected this recommendation in the Action Plan. However, the logical framework only mentions leasing and factoring. The monitoring of the effective implementation of measures should therefore be ensured.
Further develop venture capital and business angels ecosystem	●	A dedicated objective was added to the Strategy, and the logical framework targets a twofold increase of the annual financial investment volume by 2025.
Broaden financial education initiatives	●	The Strategy entails an objective on further improving financial literacy, and the OECD/INFE tool will be used for monitoring purposes.

○ Not incorporated   ◑ Partly incorporated   ● Incorporated

Table 1.6. Suggested KPIs to monitor the improvements in access to finance

KPI	Description/rationale	Baseline (2019)	Target (2025)	Source of data
SME investment in fixed assets	This indicator was suggested as impact indicator for the Priority, to replace SME productivity (now used as overall target for the Strategy). It enables to monitor the Priority as it is most directly affected by the availability of finance.	GEL 2.5 billion	15% increase	Geostat
% of companies participating in State Financing Programmes that are able to access financing from non-state sources *after* their participation in the State Financing Program	This outcome indicator was suggested to help assess the impact of State Financing Programmes.	10%	40%	GITA's report
% of training participants reporting that the skills learned at the training will help them better manage their business finances	This is an outcome indicator, suggested to replace "number of activities and events", which was rather an output indicator. To obtain the data, a simple survey among training participants could be done some time after the training, e.g. an email sent to them 3 - 6 months later.	n/a	80%	NBG's report
Actual financial literacy score for entrepreneurs	This indicator goes in line with the recommendation on collecting data on financial literacy of entrepreneurs using the OECD/INFE survey tool. As there is no baseline (no survey has been carried out before), the OECD suggested to simply use "improved level of financial literacy score for entrepreneurs".	n/a	Improved level of financial literacy score for entrepreneurs (vs score of 2021 survey)	OECD/INFE survey report
Loans with real estate collateral	This indicator gives a useful indication of the extent of pledging, and is already available on the NBG website.	GEL 19.1 billion	GEL 28.7 billion	NBG's report
Annual financial investment volume from VC and "Business angels" funds	This outcome indicator goes in line with the dedicated objective added upon OECD recommendation. To obtain data, the OECD suggested to request from VC and similar funds to report to financial regulator.	USD 0.5 million	USD 1 million	GITA's report

Note: This table only includes the KPIs that have been added to the Priority upon OECD recommendation. It does not reflect exhaustively the comments provided by the OECD, e.g. on improving KPIs that were already included in the initial draft of the logical framework. Baseline and target values are those included in the adopted version of the logical framework.

Priority 4: Promoting export growth, market access and SME internationalisation

State of play

Georgian SMEs' exports increased over the last Strategy period (+41% since 2015, despite the COVID-19 induced drop in 2020) (Figure 1.2). This growth has been driven by medium sized firms, while smaller ones have stalled. Since 2015, the share of exports generated by medium size enterprises has increased by nearly 10 percentage points (from 28.8% to 37.8%), while small firms' share has decreased by 13 percentage points (from 30.9% to 17.7%) (Geostat, 2021[47]). This rise in exports goes in line with improvements in the overall trade environment, which are reflected in international indicators such as the OECD *Trade facilitation indicators*, notably on information availability (OECD, 2019[48]). This is notably due to a number of platforms now providing up-to-date and easy-to-access information on trade requirements: the Revenue Service Customs platform offers information on the rules and administrative procedures in place, while the Unified Electronic System of Licenses, Permits and Certifications gathers information on the necessary licenses and permits in a number of domains (UNECE, 2018[49]).

Figure 1.2. Exports of Georgian firms by size

Million USD

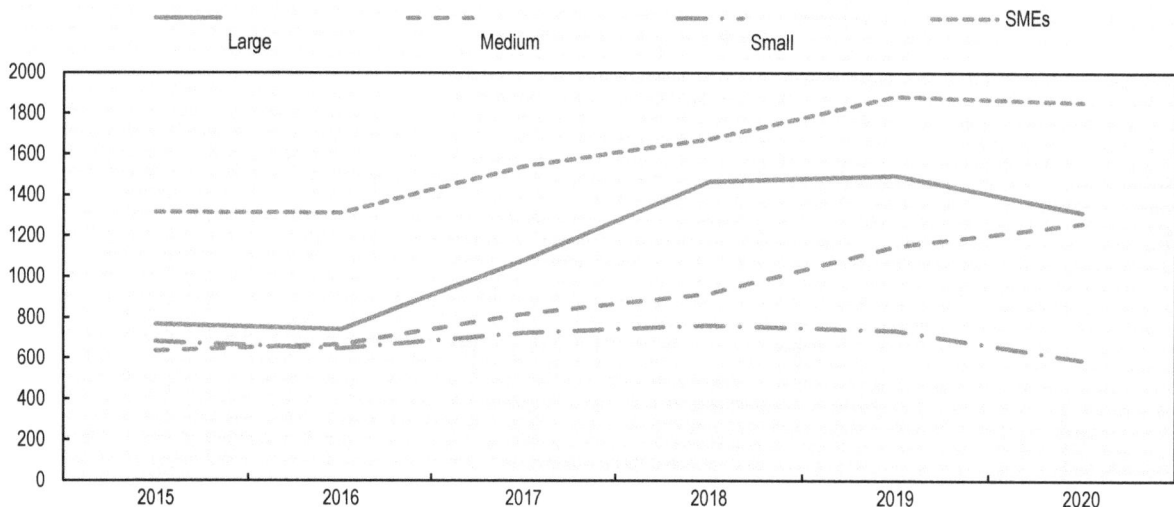

Source: (Geostat, 2021[47]).

Among the recent key achievements to foster SME internationalisation, Georgia has introduced measures to improve SMEs' knowledge of the export opportunities offered by the DCFTA and the related requirements. Indeed, the application of the DCFTA, signed in 2014 and entered into force in 2016, has been bringing Georgia closer to the EU through the gradual approximation of Georgian legislation, standards and rules to that of the EU, reducing tariffs and increasing the efficiency of customs procedures, and thereby helping Georgian firms tap into the EU's market potential[2]. However, Georgian businesses need to be aware of and stay up to date with the legislative and regulatory changes, and related requirements. To this end, DCFTA information centres, mentioned in Priority 1 above, have been established in Gori, Kutaisi, Zugdidi, Sighnaghi and Batumi, providing entrepreneurs with dedicated

---

[2] For more information on the benefits of the EU-Georgia DCFTA, see https://trade.ec.europa.eu/access-to-markets/en/content/eu-georgia-deep-and-comprehensive-free-trade-area.

trainings (e.g. on EU market standards), advisory and consulting services. 6 410 SMEs have reportedly benefitted from these (GIZ, 2020[50]).

In addition, five clusters have been created in co-operation with GIZ to help SMEs and other stakeholders from a given sector connect with one another. Priority sub-sectors have been identified to this end – apparel, film production, furniture/interior design, ICT and honey. Such clusters enable cost optimisation, and harmonisation of standards, improvement of sales, performance and skills; they also facilitate the introduction of innovations through enhanced cooperation. They also promote the internationalisation of SMEs in a variety of ways, e.g. by involving international experts and consultants, by organising international workshops to enhance member companies' skills as well as international conferences that allow for knowledge sharing and networking, and by fostering international cooperation with sectoral companies abroad.

Moreover, Enterprise Georgia has extended its assistance to SMEs seeking to export through various services, such as trainings on export management. It has also developed online training courses on export basics, available at www.tradewithgeorgia.com, and published an "export guide" for interested businesses. An export readiness test was introduced to help businesses assess their marketing abilities and competencies to access foreign markets, and adapt services based on their export capacity. The uptake of this programme remains at a nascent stage.

Although exports to the EU have been growing since 2015, Georgian firms continue to export primarily to neighbouring markets. However, in relative terms, exports to Commonwealth of Independent States (CIS) countries are declining, from over half of the total until 2019 to 45% in 2020 (Figure 1.3).

Figure 1.3. Exports of Georgian firms by country groups

Percentage of total exports, 2020

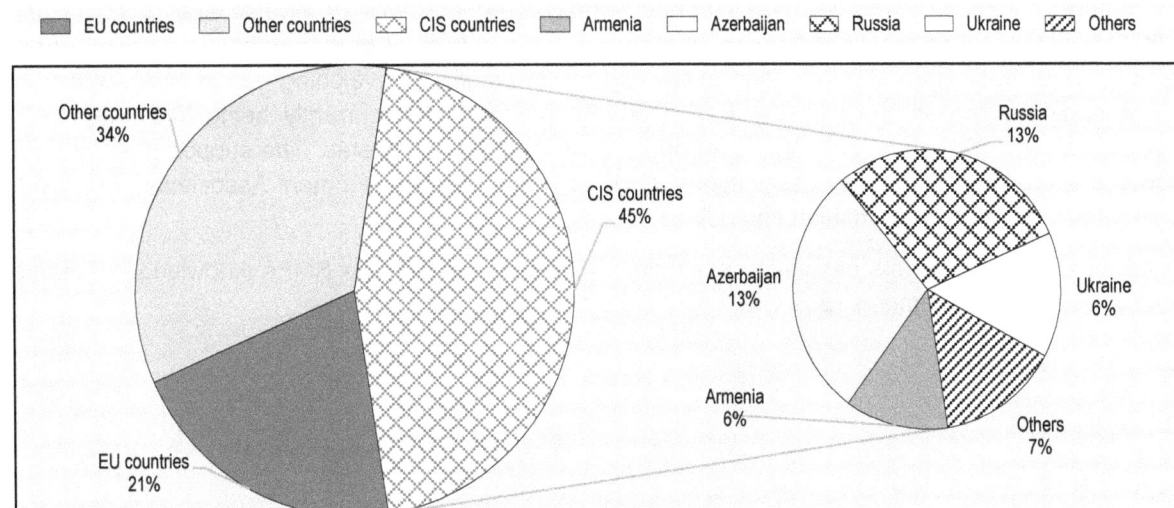

Note: CIS countries refer to Commonwealth of Independent States (Azerbaijan, Armenia, Belarus, Georgia, Kazakhstan, Kyrgyzstan, Moldova, Russia, Tajikistan, Turkmenistan, Uzbekistan and Ukraine).
Source: (Geostat, 2021[47]).

In terms of products, exports remain little diversified and mainly low-value added, with three sectors representing 80% of total exports – manufacturing (35%), wholesale and retail trade (25%), and transportation and storage (20%) in 2020. More than 50% of exports were made up by copper ores (23%), motor cars (12%), ferroalloys (7%), wine (6%), and spirituous beverages (4%) (Geostat, 2021[47]).

This issue can be partially explained by persisting information barriers: interviews with private sector associations suggested that Georgian SMEs, especially in the regions, often lack knowledge of what is needed by foreign markets, especially the EU, and what products are most exportable. Furthermore, despite progress in raising awareness of market requirements, SMEs still struggle to meet all standards and regulations due to limited human and financial resources. Yet providing timely information to exporting companies is all the more important in times of crisis (OECD, 2020[51]). Another issue lies in high shipping costs and lengthy delivery times, which impede SMEs competitiveness on international markets.

Finally, Enterprise Georgia does provide some financial help for SMEs' internationalisation, such as co-financing of participation costs in international fairs/events, and some banks offer a few trade financing options, but trade-specific financial instruments are otherwise lacking. Over the past years, the Georgian government has considered establishing an export credit agency, but it has not yet materialised. According to interviews with private sector associations, SMEs still report access to trade finance as one of the main barriers to exporting, notably due to their limited cash flow.

Way forward

Help SMEs identify market opportunities

The lack of information on demand in foreign markets still impedes SME exports, notably to the EU. In order to tackle this issue, it is essential to help Georgian SMEs improve their knowledge about market trends and competitors, to assess market needs and identify segments that they could tap. Conducting market studies would be a way to deepen the understanding of target markets, and identify niches and opportunities to foster integration in both emerging regional value chains and the EU market.

Increase advisory and training capacities to improve knowledge of market requirements

Furthermore, to improve SMEs' knowledge of foreign market requirements, Enterprise Georgia could build on the existing services mentioned above and increase the uptake of programmes. The new Strategy foresees some trainings and information sessions, but, in addition, developing export "help desks", in regions and/or online, in line with the EaP Trade Helpdesk that is currently being implemented by EU4Business (EU4Business, 2021[52]), is an option that could be considered. The support agency could outsource some skills to industry associations, such as the Export Development Association, to provide SMEs with more tailored information and advice.

Singapore for instance offers interesting examples of initiatives to improve SMEs' knowledge of market opportunities and requirements (Box 1.4).

Box 1.4. Enterprise Singapore: Go Global

Go Global is the initiative of Enterprise Singapore, the government agency for enterprise development, to foster enterprises' internationalisation. The initiative has implemented various instruments to help businesses access a new market, e.g. markets studies, capacity building, networking, and financial support. The agency has been particularly successful in providing comprehensive support on market information and in outsourcing the provision of these services.

Building knowledge of markets

The initiative offers guides, training sessions, and consultancy services to equip entrepreneurs' with the tools to carry out market studies. On one side, the Overseas Market Workshops provides first-hand experience of the market environment, by organising experts' lectures, as well as corporate and site visits. On the other side, the SME Centre Business Advisors offer tailored consultancy services to guide SMEs through the different steps of market analysis, helping them to assess which markets best fit their company. In particular, they help entrepreneurs identify priorities, and consider the main opportunities and issues, resulting from Trade agreements and tariffs regimes, as well as from potential partners.

Partnering with external stakeholders

In order to reach a higher number of companies and ensure to cover all their needs, Enterprise Singapore has partnered with the main entrepreneurial stakeholders. It relies on GlobalConnect@SBF, an initiative of Singapore Business Federation, i.e., a local business association, to provide expertise on the different markets, on how to establish operations, and how to connect with potential partners. It also collaborates with specialised SME centres to perform tailored capability assessments and provide consultancy on how to bridge the gaps. In addition to these, the agency also collaborates with some local stakeholders in China and India, two of the main markets for the country, to enhance international collaboration and ease the access to these crucial markets.

Source: (Enterprise Singapore, 2021[53]).

Help reduce SME shipping costs and time

Measures could be introduced to reduce the high shipping costs and delivery times. Indeed, while Georgian SMEs selling online may have quality products, the logistics to deliver from Georgia to EU markets lead to longer delivery times, and therefore lower competitiveness. Storing goods in warehouses in target markets is useful to this end, to have them ready to be quickly dispatched. To support that, the Strategy could include provisions on raising SMEs' awareness of such warehousing options and increasing their access thereto, e.g. by subsidising costs for first-time users. This could build on the pilot initiative currently being implemented by EU4Digital (EU4Digital, 2021[54]): the latter was launched in Armenia, Azerbaijan, Georgia, and Germany to support retailers and marketplaces to place the products for sale abroad and facilitate cross-border delivery. From Georgia, two women-led businesses participated in the pilot. As a follow-up, EU4Digital is providing additional consultations to the EaP countries on the adoption of the virtual warehouse.

Consider expanding use of trade financing options

As access to trade finance remains a major issue for SMEs, the government could foster the development of trade financing options to help firms overcome financing barriers such as the lack of cash flow and trade related risks, e.g. of non-payment when payments are made at delivery. These could be offered for instance through a range of instruments, such as export factoring, export loans, export credit insurance, or letters of credit (OECD, 2020[55]).

Develop e-commerce skills and practices

Georgia, like other countries, is experiencing a sharp increase in e-commerce as a result of widespread social distancing measures. Several initiatives have been implemented to help SMEs engage with online trade, such as the trainings on digital skills offered by the GCCI. As a follow-up to these, the latter developed a new one-off project "Free webpages for business" with the support of the Chamber of Commerce of Munich and Upper Bavaria, a competition that will select and help 100 entrepreneurs develop a personalised website free-of-charge. Building on these initiatives, additional steps could be taken – e.g. expanding digital skills courses building on the existing successful sessions, and further aligning standards with that of the EU[3].

Table 1.7. Overview of recommendations to foster SME internationalisation

Recommendation	Status	Details
Support SMEs in identifying market opportunities	●	Provisions were integrated in the Strategy to improve knowledge about market trends and competitors through market studies and other instruments.
Increase advisory and training capacities to improve knowledge of market requirements	◑	The Strategy plans training and information sessions, notably on DCFTA opportunities. To further improve SMEs' knowledge of market requirements and opportunities, Georgia could consider developing help desks and outsourcing some skills.
Help reduce SME shipping costs and time	○	Enterprise Georgia reported looking into warehousing and logistic hubs programmes, but the topic is not covered by the Strategy and no measure to create such a programme has been planned yet.
Consider expanding use of trade financing options	○	The Strategy does not foresee the expansion of trade financing tools.
Develop e-commerce skills and practices	◑	Consulting services and trainings are planned. In addition, Georgia should adopt a legal framework regulating e-commerce practices and enhance consumer protection, in line with EU standards and DCFTA requirements (see Part 2 for more detail).

○ Not incorporated　◑ Partly incorporated　● Incorporated

Table 1.8. Suggested KPIs to monitor progress in SME internationalisation

KPI	Description/rationale	Baseline (2019)	Target (2025)	Source of data
Positive feedback based on surveys of beneficiary companies	This outcome indicator was suggested to help assess whether events have helped participants establish international business relationships.	n/a	70%	LEPL Enterprise Georgia's report
% of trained participants targeting the EU market, confirming the use of trained DCFTA knowledge in daily work	This is an outcome indicator, suggested to replace "number of trainings/events", which was rather an output indicator. To obtain the data, a simple survey among training participants could be done some time after the training, e.g. an email sent to them 3 - 6 months later	n/a	60%	LEPL Enterprise Georgia's report

Note: This table only includes the KPIs that have been added to the Priority upon OECD recommendation. It does not reflect exhaustively the comments provided by the OECD, e.g. on improving KPIs that were already included in the initial draft of the logical framework. Baseline and target values are those included in the adopted version of the logical framework.

[3] For more detail on how to harmonise regulatory frameworks, develop e-commerce skills and practices, see Part 2.

Priority 5: Supporting ICT adoption, innovation and R&D for SMEs

State of play

Georgia has taken considerable steps to enhance its policy and legal framework for innovation, which has been acknowledged in the latest edition of the SMEPI (OECD et al., 2020[1]). In particular, Georgia developed an Innovation Strategy with the support of USAID in 2019. The Agency assessed the country's innovation ecosystem and identified its strengths and weaknesses, notably its relatively weak talent pool, low research capability, limited access to finance and lack of support for high-growth entrepreneurs (USAID Georgia, 2019[56]). In June 2016, Georgia also adopted a *Law on Innovations* which defines the various structures to support innovation (incubators, accelerators, technology transfer centres, etc.), and sets principles for innovation financing and commercialisation (Government of Georgia, 2016[57]).

In addition to these framework improvements, the innovation infrastructure in the country has been expanded. Georgia now benefits from above-mentioned FabLabs, three Techparks, five innovation centres and two regional innovation hubs, ensuring regional coverage. GITA plans to open four additional regional innovation hubs and innovation centres (GITA, 2021[58]). A network of innovation laboratories is also being developed: three have been created so far in co-operation with universities and the private sector, offering trainings and events (e.g. hackathons) to enhance digital skills as well as working spaces for start-ups.

Table 1.9. Types of innovation infrastructure in Georgia

	Description	Number	Coverage
FabLabs	Based on a concept from the MIT, offer individuals the infrastructure to carry out digital fabrication, i.e. designing and producing by using digital tools.	22	9 in Tbilisi , 2 in Batumi, 2 in Kutaisi, 1 in Mestia, 1 in Gurjaani, 1 in Akhaltsikhe, 1 in Kobuleti, 1 in Tsalenjikha, 1 in Poti, 1 in Ambrolauri, 1 in Rustavi, 1 in Zugdidi
Techparks	Gather technological, educational and professional resources, including incubators, training centres, laboratories, and working spaces.	3	Tbilisi, Zugdidi, and Telavi
Innovation centres	Offer the same services as techparks, but locally and on a smaller scale.	5 (2 are planned to open)	Kharagauli, Baghdadi, Choporti, Akhmeta, and Rukhi
Regional innovation hubs	Aim at connecting innovation centres with each other, while offering industrial, well-equipped innovation laboratories.	2 (2 are planned to open in Batumi and Tbilisi)	Zugdidi and Telavi
Innovation laboratories (innovation labs)	Help young people develop the necessary skills to create innovative businesses.	3	GeoLab, Gamelab Iliauni and CG multilab GIP: all located in Tbilisi

Source: (FabLab Georgia, 2021[25]), (GITA, 2021[58]), (GITA, 2021[59]), (GeoLab, 2021[60]), (ILIA State University, 2021[61]), and (GIPA, 2021[62]).

GITA has also introduced a wide range of financing tools to support innovation, in particular with the help of the World Bank GENIE project (Georgian National Innovation Ecosystem). These include a co-financing grant programme (max. 90% of the project's overall budget) with a GEL 2 mln annual budget (approx. USD 640 000), which attracts thousands of applications each year and benefitting 95 start-ups with grants up to GEL 100 000 (USD 32 000) as of July 2021. Another initiative offers to co-finance up to 50% of a project, up to GEL 650 000 (USD 208 000). Start-ups can also be supported in the development of a prototype with micro-grants. Information on these programmes is easily accessible online on a dedicated website, grants.gov.ge[4].

Despite the initiatives described above, Georgia still has room for improvement to strengthen its innovation ecosystem and innovation support to SMEs, as reflected in international rankings such as the (World Economic Forum, 2019[27]) *Global Competitiveness Index* and INSEAD's *Global Innovation Index* 2020.

Spending on Research & Development remains relatively low in Georgia, at 0.3% of GDP against 2.5% in the OECD (OECD, 2021[63]). In that regard, it can also be noted that smaller companies tend to invest less: only 4.4% of small Georgian companies and 18.4% of medium ones reported R&D expenditures in 2019, while 21.6% of large firms did so (World Bank, 2019[28]). Only 2.1% of GERD (Gross Expenditure on R&D) was financed by businesses in 2020, against 65% in EU countries (INSEAD, 2020[64]).

Moreover, while GITA has been developing a wide range of initiatives to foster the emergence and scaling up of innovative firms and digital start-ups, support for innovation in non-IT sectors is still limited and could be further developed, as further explained in Part 2. This dimension of the Strategy is primarily oriented towards ICT and Internet access, which is one of the Government's current policy priorities, rather than innovation and R&D. Yet innovation should not be understood merely as the introduction of a new digital product, just like digitalisation is not only about the IT sector or technology adoption. Helping all firms, regardless of their sector, be more innovative and, where relevant, digitalise some processes and/or products and services, would increase their resilience to future shocks – especially SMEs.

Way forward

Provide indirect financial incentives for innovation

GITA's financial support to innovative firms could be complemented by indirect or expenditure-based financial incentives to firms. Hyper-depreciation schemes and/or tax credits can be used to foster businesses' investment in technology, and have proven successful in OECD/EU countries. As an example, Italy has introduced such measures through its Impresa 4.0 National Plan: firms could benefit from a 150% increase in the ordinary depreciation deduction for investments in certain industrial equipment (40% in the case of super-depreciation), which substantially reduces the tax burden over the years. In addition, a tax credit of 50% is applied for firms that increased their R&D expenditure (Ministry of Economic Development of Italy, 2021[65]).

Introduce financing tools targeted at supporting the digital transformation in non-IT sectors

Existing financing tools introduced by GITA focus mainly on the IT sector. Yet the digital transformation of all firms, including in non-IT sectors, can yield significant benefits (see Part 2). Further measures could therefore be considered – Part 2 outlines a blueprint for policymakers as well as detailed recommendations for that purpose (see from page 84 onwards). The Digitalisation Pilot of the EU's Competitiveness of Enterprises and SMEs (COSME) Loan Guarantee Facility could serve as a reference for the classification of eligible processes to receive funding for digital transformation initiatives.

Consider demand-side policies

Moreover, demand-side innovation policies could be leveraged, as they spur innovation without requiring additional programme spending. In terms of public procurement, for instance, upgrading standards by introducing functional specifications in the process, instead of letting bidders compete only on cost, could provide more incentives for the diffusion of innovations. Moldova for instance has integrated such an objective in its public procurement framework through the adoption of its 2015 *Law on Public Procurement*.

---

[4] Further detail are available in Part 2, Box 2.3

These incentives should go along with safeguards against corruption risks, as public procurement is one of the government activities most vulnerable to corruption (OECD, 2016[66]) (OECD, 2017[67]).

Deepen research / industry linkages

Finally, university/industry research collaboration is still highlighted as one of the main weaknesses of Georgia's innovation framework (INSEAD, 2020[68]). A dedicated objective was added to the Strategy upon OECD recommendation. Specific actions could be considered during the implementation of the Strategy. Measures could include monitoring GITA's Technology Transfer Pilot Programme, a promising initiative launched in 2019 with the help of the EU and World Bank to support the commercialisation of scientific projects and partnering with public universities and research institutions, and, if positive, ensuring its continuation.

In addition to these, it should be noted that innovation appears as a crosscutting dimension, and can thus be fostered by policy recommendations described in other priorities of the Strategy – such as regulatory sandboxes (Box 1.3).

Table 1.10. Overview of recommendations to support innovation and R&D among SMEs

Recommendation	Status	Details
Provide indirect financial incentives for innovation	○	Such incentives have not been included in the Strategy.
Introduce financing tools targeted at supporting the digital transformation in non-IT sectors	◑	A reference to supporting the digital transformation of SMEs was added to the Strategy, but only a few non-financial tools are foreseen (e.g. trainings on digital skills). The government could still consider introducing dedicated financial tools in future action plans upon availability of public funds. More details on potential support measures are outlined in Part 2.
Consider demand-side policies	○	The Strategy does not foresee demand-side policies.
Deepen research / industry linkages	●	An objective on *deepening research/industry linkages* was added to the Strategy. GITA reported plans to set up a national technology transfer office to support the commercialisation of projects developed in universities and research labs.

○ Not incorporated   ◑ Partly incorporated   ● Incorporated

Table 1.11. Suggested KPIs to monitor innovation policies

KPI	Description/rationale	Baseline (2019)	Target (2025)	Source of data
Number of SMEs that have developed (at prototype level) an innovative product or service among beneficiaries of State support programmes	This outcome indicator was suggested to assess the impact of State support programmes. The number could be tracked with a survey of programme participants at the beginning of the programme, followed by yearly updates.	27	100	GITA's report
Number of tech transfer projects brought to commercialisation stage	This outcome indicator was suggested for the objective on deepening research/industry linkages, which was added as recommended by the OECD.	0	Minimum 1	GITA's report

Note: This table only includes the KPIs that have been added to the Priority upon OECD recommendation. It does not reflect exhaustively the comments provided by the OECD, e.g. on improving KPIs that were already included in the initial draft of the logical framework. Baseline and target values are those included in the adopted version of the logical framework.

Priority 6: Encouraging women's entrepreneurship

State of play

Over the past years, Georgia has been paying increasing attention to women's entrepreneurship and its role in the country's economic and social development. Women's entrepreneurship is now a stand-alone priority of the new SME Development Strategy. The overall environment has improved for female entrepreneurs, as reflected in international rankings: in the Global Gender Gap Report 2021, for instance, Georgia moved up 25 places from the previous year (World Economic Forum, 2021[69]).

This is due to various policy measures taken in recent years. The institutional framework has been strengthened with the creation of a sub-committee on women entrepreneurship within the Private Sector Development Advisory Council in early 2018, which complements the Inter-Agency Commission for Gender Equality established in 2017. The sub-committee aims at better identifying women entrepreneurs' needs and holds several sessions throughout the year, gathering women entrepreneurs from state agencies and representatives from the Women in Business Association. As for the legal framework, a number of recently enacted laws, such as the Labour Reform adopted in September 2020, have included gender-sensitive provisions. Moreover, the recent changes to the electoral code introduced quotas in parliament and local assemblies, to enhance women's political involvement.

In addition, women's participation in governmental programmes has also increased: as an example, in 2018, 45% of participants in the "Produce in Georgia" programme were women, against 40% in 2016. Some of the measures taken by the Ministry of Economy and Sustainable Development in response to the COVID-19 crisis have enhanced this trend, as preconditions to enter economic support programmes were alleviated and women applicants benefitted from extra points in their applications' assessment (UNDP, 2020[70]).

Georgian women have valuable assets, such as their high levels of education, which are comparable to men's (Figure 1.4). et this is not reflected in employability, wages and entrepreneurship, where considerable gender gaps persist. Women's potential remains untapped because of persisting barriers: in terms of access to finance, for instance, data show that they encounter more difficulties when trying to get a loan than men do, especially in regions/outside the capital city, often because they lack collateral demanded by banks (Figure 1.5). They also appear disadvantaged in terms of entrepreneurial skills and networks, which they struggle to get access to (Griessbach and Ettl, 2020[71]).

Figure 1.4. Educational attainment by gender, 2020

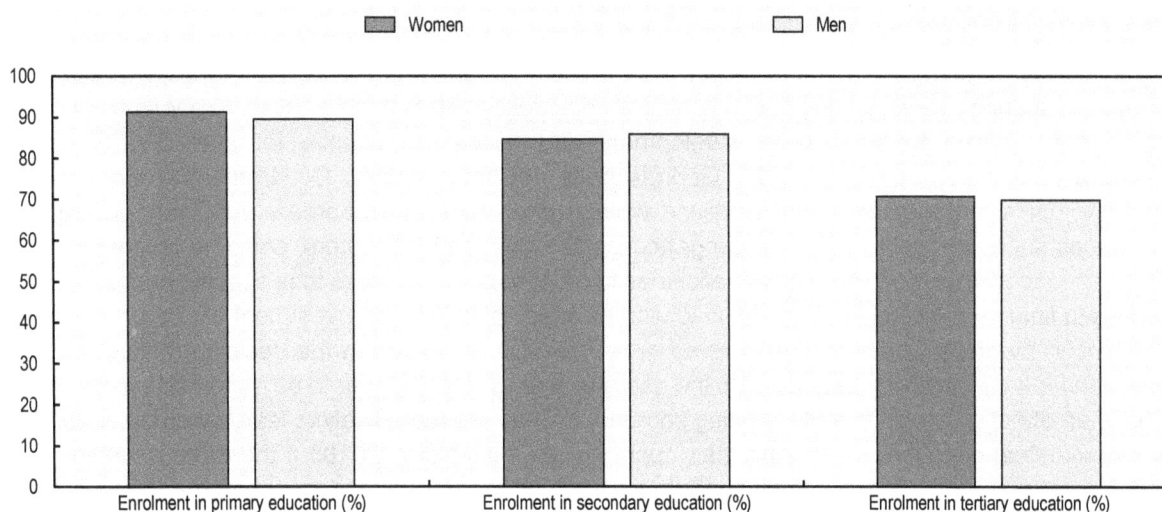

Source: (World Economic Forum, 2021[69]).

Figure 1.5. Barriers in access to bank finance, by gender, 2019

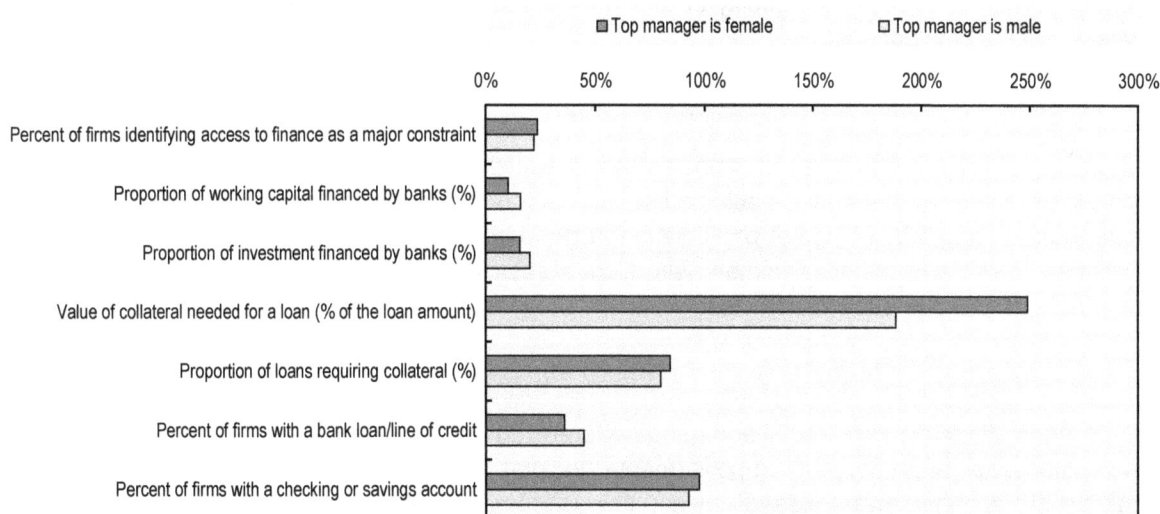

Source: (World Bank, 2019[28]).

Moreover, the underrepresentation of women in STEM (science, technology, engineering and mathematics) fields remains an issue. The percentage of female Georgian tertiary education graduates in STEM fields is only 19%, against 53% men (World Economic Forum, 2021[69]). Similarly, only 12% of women are employed in these sectors, compared to 30% globally (EU4Digital, 2020[72]).

Finally, women have been particularly affected by the COVID-19 crisis, largely because many were working in hard hit sectors such as tourism and trade. In addition, their burden of housework, which was already disproportionate, has substantially increased as a result of containment measures: 42% of women reported spending more time on domestic tasks, while this is the case for only 35% of men (UN Women, 2020[73]).

Way forward

Develop gender-tailored support programmes

A few initiatives targeting women specifically exist in Georgia, such as the EBRD's Women in Business programme, offering events, workshops, and facilitated access to funding, and USAID/Georgia and Crystal Fund initiative, which fostered skills development and access to finance for over 2 000 women entrepreneurs between 2015 and 2020. Georgia does not have specific Government programmes to support women's entrepreneurship. Yet, since women often face more barriers than men do, support programmes such as training and mentoring, access to loans, and incubators, could be tailored to them and delivered to women-only group of beneficiaries in order to better address their specific needs. In terms of access to finance for instance, in addition to women's lack of collateral, investment allocation is likely to be influenced by gender bias, all the more so given the lack of women in the decision-making process (Innovation Finance Advisory, 2020[74]). On the demand side, women appear to be more risk averse, which can have an effect on the choice of financing sources, as they are more likely to lean towards self-funding over external financing, thereby limiting their opportunities. Halabisky (2018[75]) therefore underlines the importance of promoting financing solutions that specifically target women to overcome these gender-based challenges. Governments can for example invest in women-led VC in exchange of an equity stake, as done for instance in Ireland with the Competitive Start Fund for Female Entrepreneurs. This fund provides an equity investment of up to 10% and EUR 50 000, aimed at helping women starting a company in selected sectors scale up. A similar gender bias affects angel investments, i.e. early stage investments offered by individuals. To counter it, governments can for instance step up financial education training for women, to help them improve the quality of their loan applications and financial pitches, and raise their awareness of financing options.

Improve data collection on gender-related issues

In order to tailor support measures to women's needs, enriching databases and deepening research on the topic is essential. To that end, it would be beneficial to conduct regular studies on barriers to women's entrepreneurship and labour market participation in general, in order to monitor the impact of existing programmes, track the evolution of women's situation, assess the policy impact, and identify and remaining challenges to adapt state support accordingly.

Step up awareness-raising activities to bridge the gender gap

Finally, women still suffer from social and gender stereotypes (Griessbach and Ettl, 2020[71]). In addition to the popularisation of the Women Empowerment Principles foreseen in the Strategy, the Government of Georgia could plan public awareness-raising campaigns promoting gender equality and targeting the whole society, especially in rural areas. These could for instance showcase successful women entrepreneurs from different backgrounds and sectors (Halabisky, 2018[75]). Additional measures could be implemented to encourage women to go into STEM education, building on GITA's events for women in tech. Finland, for instance, has developed such targeted programmes, which also include financing tools and mentoring (EU4Digital, 2020[72]).

Table 1.12. Overview of recommendations to support women's entrepreneurship

Recommendation	Status	Details
Develop gender-tailored support programmes	○	The Strategy does not foresee the development of gender-specific programmes. However, one of its objectives aims at increasing women's participation in existing programmes, which is a welcome measure.
Improve data collection on gender-related issues	◐	The Strategy now specifies that SME statistics by gender will be improved, and plans to monitor women's participation in support programmes. In addition, future action plans could include conducting regular studies on barriers to women's entrepreneurship, to produce some qualitative analysis.
Step up awareness-raising activities to bridge the gender gap	◐	This recommendation has been reflected in the action plan, and the Strategy now emphasises the importance of promoting women's participation in STEM fields. Information sessions on women's empowerment principles are planned, but additional activities, as outlined above, could be considered.

○ Not incorporated   ◐ Partly incorporated   ● Incorporated

Table 1.13. Suggested KPIs to monitor improvements in policy support to women's entrepreneurship

KPI	Description/rationale	Baseline (2019)	Target (2025)	Source of data
% of training participants on women's empowerment principles reporting that the content learned will help them promote gender equality in their business	This is an outcome indicator, suggested to complement "number of information sessions", which was rather an output indicator. To obtain the data, a simple survey among training participants could be done some time after the training, e.g. an email sent to them 3 - 6 months later	n/a	65%	LEPL Enterprise Georgia's report
% of training participants on digital skills reporting that the skills learned at the training will help them improve their business practice	This is an outcome indicator, suggested to replace "number of women participants in trainings", which was rather an output indicator. To obtain the data, a simple survey among training participants could be done some time after the training, e.g. an email sent to them 3 - 6 months later	n/a	70%	Progress report of the SME Development Strategy
% of training participants on capacity building of state institutions reporting that the skills and knowledge received will be useful in their activities in terms of gender-based approaches	This is an outcome indicator, suggested to replace "number of trainings", which was rather an output indicator. To obtain the data, a simple survey among training participants could be done some time after the training, e.g. an email sent to them 3 - 6 months later	n/a	70%	Progress report of the SME Development Strategy

Note: This table only includes the KPIs that have been added to the Priority upon OECD recommendation. It does not reflect exhaustively the comments provided by the OECD, e.g. on improving KPIs that were already included in the initial draft of the logical framework. Baseline and target values are those included in the adopted version of the logical framework.

Priority 7: Developing the green economy

State of play

For the first time, green growth is a stand-alone priority in the new SME Strategy. This reflects the increasing efforts made by the Georgian government to integrate environmental considerations in the economic development and align its environmental policies with international standards. Under the last Strategy, several policy documents defining overall environmental priorities and objectives were adopted, such as the Third National Environmental Action Programme 2017-2021 and the Waste Management

Strategy 2016-2030. A number of measures that were implemented following these policies have resulted in an overall improvement of the green economy indicators in the (OECD et al., 2020[11]) *SME Policy Index* compared to the 2016 edition (from 2.48 to 3.05).

Georgia has also implemented green measures in response to the COVID-19 pandemic, including measures improving air quality, energy consumption, agricultural practices, and waste management, and, unlike most countries in the region, COVID-19 policies in Georgia did not entail potentially negative environmental implications, such as the reduction of environmental checks, the slowdown of green policy reforms or the re-allocation of funds towards healthcare (OECD, 2021[76]). In 2021, Georgia updated a report on Nationally Determined Contributions report that presents more ambitious measures to promote the low carbon development of the economy. Moreover, the Georgian government is currently working on a Green Growth concept, strategy and action plan, in cooperation with international partners such as the EU4Environment programme. Additional plans targeting specific sectors are being drafted, such as tourism with Georgia's ecotourism strategy for 2020-2030, which aims at positioning the country as a leader in the field. Other sectoral strategies include green provisions, e.g. Georgia's Agriculture and Rural Development Strategy 2021-2027, which foresees measures fostering sustainable practices in farming and forestry, as well as promotion of application of energy-efficient and renewable energy technologies in rural households and enterprises.

Despite these efforts, challenges remain. Finalising the long-awaited Green Growth Strategy would be essential to ensure a comprehensive and co-ordinated approach towards greening. At this stage, SME-specific greening policies remain fragmented and only focus on some sectors. Yet supporting SMEs' green transition should be among the key priorities for the country, since their aggregate impacts are considerably greater than those of large firms: even if SMEs have a lower environmental footprint than large firms individually, their preponderance makes their aggregate impact considerably greater. Adopting greener practices can also have a positive economic impact on firms themselves, as it would also help businesses cut operational costs, e.g. by minimising the amount of energy used and of waste generated. In addition, SMEs can support the greening of the economy by offering green products and services. In that regard, this priority is closely linked to the one on innovation, for start-ups can be a driver of green innovations.

Way forward

Set more concrete definitions and goals in the Strategy document

Providing efficient support to Georgian SMEs requires a strategic vision for green growth. The new SME Strategy offers an important opportunity to provide that vision and sets out a clear ambition for the legislative framework and specific support. Clarifications have been added to the Strategy regarding the areas of the economy to be covered by the upcoming Green Growth Strategy and legislative framework, but the document could have benefitted from more details, e.g. on the timeline. Moving forward, the government should ensure that the Green Growth Strategy sets clear definitions, timeframe and targets.

Task Enterprise Georgia with leading support for SME greening

Along with an overarching vision, measures for SME greening would benefit from a more co-ordinated approach. Enterprise Georgia is currently working on incorporating support to green economy in its programmes as part of the IBRD Georgia Relief and Recovery for MSMEs (Micro Small and Medium Enterprises) project. Building on this, it could play a role of a single agency responsible for co-ordinating of different actors in greening efforts and acting as a point of contact for SMEs. Embedding the Green Economy Development in its portfolio would provide a conduit to greatly improve companies' awareness of the benefits and opportunities of the Green Economy, while providing a means for direct support to interested SMEs.

Target efficiency measures to SMEs

In the area of energy efficiency, Georgia is working on the adoption of an updated Energy Efficiency Directive and National Energy and Climate Plan. However, small enterprises often have trouble accessing these types of programmes, unless the programme is designed in such a way to facilitate it. Some of the efficiency measures foreseen should therefore be tailored to SMEs specifically. As access to bank finance remains one of the main issues, the measures should try to tackle this issue, for instance by developing loans from alternative sources such as microfinance institutions, institutional investors, and non-financial sector corporations (OECD, 2018[77]). A first step towards this direction was already taken in 2019 with the launch of the EBRD's "Green Economy Financing Facility" that supports local partner banks in making loans available for SMEs (Green Economy Financing Facility, 2019[78]). Moreover, the Strategy provides for the development of a legislative framework, including in the area of energy efficiency, but without further specification. More detail could have been included, e.g. on regulatory improvements: regulatory tools are a useful way to encourage SMEs to improve their environmental performance. Those tools might include, for example, reduced environmental inspections for those SMEs that implement environmental management systems as well as a shift to general binding rules for sectors like agriculture (OECD, 2018[79]). These could be considered in future action plans.

Build capacity and awareness of opportunities from green economy

Finally, raising awareness of opportunities among Georgian SMEs is of crucial importance, as they are often not conscious of the benefits to going green, and that it can make economic sense in the long term to invest in eco-innovative approaches. In that regard, the Strategy plans several information meetings, notably on eco-innovation. As part of the EU4Environment programme and in partnership with international organisations, Georgia is developing awareness-raising initiatives such as workshops, seminars and conferences, notably with regard to energy- and resource efficiency, clean production and green finance. Additional tools could complement these, such as broader communication and tools for information provision, working with business associations as well as collaboration with universities and other educational centres.

Table 1.14. Overview of recommendations to develop the green economy

Recommendation	Status	Details
Set more concrete definitions and goals in the Strategy document	◑	The objectives on developing a green growth Strategy and a legislative framework now benefit from more details on the areas to be covered, but the government should ensure that clear definitions and targets are set in future policy documents, such as the action plans and Green Growth Strategy.
Task Enterprise Georgia with leading support for SME greening	○	Although Enterprise Georgia is working on stepping up its support to the green economy, the Strategy does not plan to task any stakeholder with leading support for SME greening.
Target efficiency measures to SMEs	◑	The Strategy foresees the development of an effective legislative framework, including in the area of energy efficiency, but more details could have been added. Regulatory improvements for SMEs could be considered during the implementation period.
Build capacity and awareness of opportunities from green economy	◑	Information sessions on eco-innovation are planned, and their impact on SMEs will be monitored. Additional tools could complement this approach, as outlined above.

○ Not incorporated   ◑ Partly incorporated   ● Incorporated

Table 1.15. Suggested KPIs to monitor progress in SME greening

KPI	Description/rationale	Baseline (2019)	Target (2025)	Source of data
Number of companies with which information meetings were held	This indicator was suggested to replace the "number of information meetings", in order to track SMEs' participation in them.	n/a	Information session with no less than 100 companies	LEPL Enterprise Georgia's report
% of training graduates who consider that the skills acquired will help them conduct environmental protection activities	This is an outcome indicator, suggested to replace "number of trainings", which was rather an output indicator. To obtain the data, a simple survey among training participants could be done some time after the training, e.g. an email sent to them 3 - 6 months later	n/a	60% training graduates	Progress report of the SME Development Strategy

Note: This table only includes the KPIs that have been added to the Priority upon OECD recommendation. It does not reflect exhaustively the comments provided by the OECD, e.g. on improving KPIs that were already included in the initial draft of the logical framework. Baseline and target values are those included in the adopted version of the logical framework.

2 Accelerating the digital transformation of SMEs

Digitalisation can bring significant benefits to economies and societies. In particular, for SMEs, it can help increase firm productivity through easier access to strategic resources, broaden the customer base and market access, achieve scale and capitalise on network effects. This chapter delves deeper into the ways Georgia can accelerate the digital transformation of the SME sector. It provides an overview of the current state of play in terms of framework conditions, such as broadband connectivity, the regulatory environment and digital literacy, and SME digitalisation. To this end, it looks at past policy achievements and upcoming measures. The last section provides further policy options to support the digital transformation of SMEs.

Why SME digitalisation matters

Digitalisation offers countless new opportunities for businesses

Digitalisation can be defined as "the use of digital technologies, data and interconnections that result in new activities or changes to existing ones" (OECD, 2019[80]). Digital technologies have been developing at an ever-increasing pace since the advent of computers and the creation of the World Wide Web, offering individuals, governments and businesses a wide range of new tools (Table 2.1). Their use in turn can have profound economic and societal effects, commonly referred to as digital transformation (OECD, 2019[80]).

Several studies investigated the effects of the adoption of digital technologies on businesses' performance and identified a substantial increase in productivity as the result of the digital transformation.[5] This can happen through different channels, ranging from increasing efficiency of operations to reaching a wider set of customers through improved marketing and sales. By adopting technologies such as advanced data analytics, resource planning software, and automation, businesses can improve quality at lower cost. Moreover, by using digital solutions to analyse consumers' online shopping behaviour, preferences and social media activity, enterprises can gain better insights and tailor more effective marketing messages (BCG, 2020[81]). Depending on the firm's characteristics, and notably on the sector of activity, digital tools can respond to specific needs (Table 2.1) provides a list of selected technologies that can be adopted by SMEs and an example of their potential applications. As illustrated by the example of the construction sector in Box 2.1 digital instruments can serve different functions tailored to the company's level of digitalisation.

Moreover, digitalisation can foster overall improvements in the business environment, as digital tools offer a variety of solutions to strengthen the rule of law, increase transparency, and limit corruption. For example, the use of e-signatures and digital authentication services improve security in transactions with public authorities, while data analytics can support applicants' integrity check during public procurements biddings (Santiso, 2021[82]). The digitalisation of public services, including that of administrative processes, limits the opportunities for corruption and increases reliability since it reduces intermediaries and the use of paper. Within SMEs, technology can help increase transparency and compliance to rules, as it allows to make data publicly available, and provides instruments such as e-invoicing that ease the process of tax declaration and reduce mistakes (World Economic Forum, 2020[83]).

Nonetheless, businesses cannot overlook the many risks and challenges digitalisation poses, such as cybersecurity threats and privacy issues relating to consumers' data. This applies to both established technologies, such as digital payments, and emerging ones: artificial intelligence (AI), for instance, raises ethical questions that require policymakers to set a regulatory framework, as well as objectives and values to observe (OECD, 2019[84]). The Internet of Things (IoT) offers another example, as its use raises increasing privacy/security concerns (OECD, 2018[85]). Understanding all the potential sources of risk and identifying strategies to address them are integral and fundamental parts of the digitalisation process (Deloitte, 2018[86]). Policymakers should therefore ensure that these concerns are taken into account and addressed when designing digitalisation policies.

---

[5] See for example Gal et al. (2019[152])

Table 2.1. Selected established and emerging digital solutions

Technology	Description	Selected examples of application
Customer-Relations Management (CRM)	This software enhances the management of front-office functions, by managing firms' interactions with customers.	Coordination platforms: stakeholders can be put in direct contact and are constantly updated about the project's progression.
Cloud Computing (CC)	ICT services accessed over the internet, including services, storage, network components, and software applications.	Cloud Accounting: multiple users can simultaneously update information, which allows fastening the process and accessibility.
Supply-Chain Management (SCM)	Used for managing the flow of goods and services, it concerns processes that transform raw materials into final products	Supervisory Control and Data Acquisition (SCADA) Plant Management: integrated platform to monitor equipment and resources across the production line.
E-commerce	It refers to the sale or purchase of goods or services conducted over computer networks by methods designed specifically for the purpose of receiving or placing orders.	E-commerce platforms: they ease the purchase process, increase product visibility and allow reaching a larger number of customers.
Electronic Invoicing	It supports compliance-by-design approaches through standardised formats, which allow for a reduction of administrative work and human mistakes (e.g. typos) in the preparation of tax declarations and billing, fostering the respect and integration of rules.	E-Invoice Management: generate invoices electronically, avoiding the use of paper and thereby increasing security and compliance with existing legislations.
Enterprise Resource Planning (ERP)	Such software allows integrating different business activities, by storing and managing information flows. As a result, business functions are automated, thereby facilitating back-office functions and strategic planning.	Asset Inventory Management: allows monitoring inventories, thereby limiting the risk of overproduction and waste.
Radio Frequency Identification (RFID)	Allow near-field communication and are used for product identification, person identification or access control, monitoring and control of industrial production, supply chain inventory tracking and tracing, service maintenance information management, or payment applications.	Warehouse Management: tracking of assets to reduce the risk of loss, and increase efficiency in shipment
5G	This new wireless technology provides up to 200 times faster connectivity than the current 4G network, while allowing the simultaneous connection of billions of devices, and machine-to-machine communications.	Virtual Reality for Simulation: they allow visualising finalised product, improving training, and easing design processes. Although they are already being used, the speed of 5G will improve user experience, making it more realistic and effective, and prompting an increase in diffusion and usage.
IoT	Devices that can be controlled and handled through the Internet, with or without the active involvement of a human being. It is likely to increase firms' capacity for simulation, prototyping, decision making and automation.	Overall Equipment Effectiveness: it enables to constantly monitor the equipment to ensure its effectiveness.
Big Data Analytics	They allow for the analysis of a vast amount of data, which can be key in supporting decision-making as it allows tailoring the supply of products and services to the demand.	Centralised Platform with Data Analytics: it allows identifying market opportunities, making data-driven planning and decisions, improving process efficiency.
AI	The ability of machine systems to learn and apply the acquired knowledge by carrying out intelligent behaviour. They can perform different cognitive tasks with a wide range of applications.	Efficient Energy Management: digital sensors to monitor energy consumption, which allow predicting energy needs and hence reduce waste and costs.
Blockchain	It is a shared ledger of transactions between parties in a network, not controlled by a single central authority, where regular updates maintain all the copies identical and verifiable by all the participants at all times. Depending on who is able to view it, they can be public or private, while they can be permissioned or permissionless, depending on whether users need permission to write.	Blockchain for Trade Documentation: end-to-end exchange of documents enabled by blockchain, increasing transaction security and transparency among all stakeholders.

Source: (OECD, 2011[87]), (OECD, 2014[88]), (OECD, 2021[89]), (OECD, 2018[90]), (Infocomm Media Development Authority, 2021[36]), and (Intel, 2021[91]).

Box 2.1. Example: Stages of adopting digital solutions by a construction company

Stage 1

The first stage should focus on exploiting digital tools to automate and strengthen basic capabilities, as well as to optimise operations through better cooperation. Instruments such as Building Information Modelling (BIM), a tool based on different technologies, and 3D Modelling, can improve visualisation and analysis capacities, easing project design. ERP tools such as collaboration platforms allow contributors to easily access each other's work, constantly remaining up-to-date on the progresses.

Stage 2

In the second stage, the target shifts to implementing integrated ecosystems and streamlining processes to further increase coordination and facilitate project management. To this aim, BIM for Facilities Management, an ERP technology, automates the maintenance of equipment and facilities, and allows to easily prevent future issues. Built Environment Digital Platforms, another type of ERP based tool, enables contributors to report issues and keep track of their resolution, and connects the partners to a large number of suppliers, making the choice of raw materials faster.

Stage 3

In this stage, the automation of operations is widened to new, more complex tasks, which allows centralising the control of all the aspects of project implementation, increasing optimisation. Blockchain technology allows having a constantly updated and trustable overview of the project's advancements. Data analytics, with the support of AI, can provide essential information on the project's most common risks and usual implementation practices, decreasing costs and increasing security. Robotics can also be adopted to support construction work, avoiding repetitive tasks and leaving more time for individuals to perform jobs with higher value-added.

Note: Example based on the industry plan for the construction sector created by Singapore's *SMEs Go Digital* Initiative.
Source: (European Construction Sector Observatory, 2021[92]) and (Infocomm Media Development Authority, 2021[93]).

With regard to the business sector, digitalisation is a major driver of structural transformation. On the one hand, technologies and the profound changes they generate by enabling new ways of working, collaborating and organising processes, create new market opportunities that firms can tap into and unlock new business models. As a result, digital-by-default firms have been emerging: a number of Georgian fast-growing digital start-ups has flourished over the past years, such as B2C.ge, a firm helping other businesses set up their online shops (more examples are detailed in Table 2.3). These are, however, only a small part of the picture. More importantly, digitalisation is also an opportunity to bring incremental changes in more "traditional" sectors, e.g. by optimising processes, products (for instance using data analysis to get consumer insights), improving customer outreach and entering new markets via e-commerce practices. ERP technologies can support sectors that engage with trade such as wholesale retail and agriculture to fasten transactions and reduce costs, e.g. by allowing monitoring inventories, thereby limiting the risk of overproduction and waste. In addition to this, the use of digital tools such as e-invoices and e-payments fosters an increase in transaction security. The use of CRM platforms can play an important role in improving coordination in different sectors, notably in construction and agriculture, two major fields for the Georgian economy. For the first one, it enables the different project contributors to be constantly up-to-date with the current developments, while, in the agricultural domain, it promotes direct contacts between local farmers and global distributors. These are only some examples of how digital tools could bring improvements to a number of traditional sectors.

The COVID-19 crisis has provided strong incentives to accelerate the digital transformation, as governments, businesses and individuals have been forced to operate remotely and have therefore increased the share of tasks carried out using online platforms. Successive lockdowns and long-lasting social distancing measures have led to a sharp decline in mobility: use of public transport hubs fell by up to 78% in April 2020 compared to baseline[6], and visits to workplaces by up to 81% (Google LLC, 2021[94]). As of end August 2021, although Georgia has not reintroduced stricter containment measures despite the new wave of infections, figures have not yet returned to normal, registering 14% and 27% decreases for visits to transit stations and workplaces, respectively. Citizens have been increasingly interacting online, while schools have had to resort to distance learning. Businesses also had to show flexibility and adapt by switching to teleworking and moving activities online: by autumn 2020, over a third of Georgian firms had started or increased online business activities (Figure 2.1), while traffic to online shops more than tripled between 2019 and 2021, reflecting changes in consumer habits that are likely to persist (Galt & Taggart, 2021[95]). Likewise, Georgians have significantly increased their use of e-government services: while the authorities have almost doubled the number of services made available on the dedicated portal my.gov.ge, which reached 700 in 2020, the use of these services has increased by more than 9 times (OECD, 2021[96])

Figure 2.1. COVID-19 impact on businesses' online activity, by firm size

Percentage of firms that started or increased online business activity in response to COVID-19 outbreak

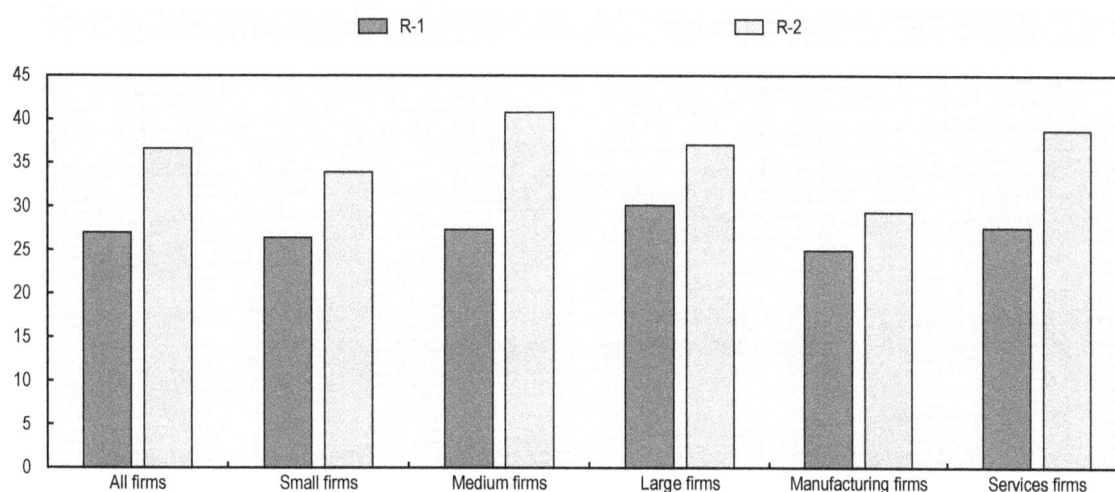

Note: R-1 corresponds to the results of the follow-up survey carried out in June 2020, R-2 to the one conducted in October/November 2020.
Source: (World Bank, 2020[15]).

The potential of digitalisation remains untapped, especially among SMEs

Although the use of digital technologies and services has been increasing, people and organisations have not yet reaped the full potential of digitalisation (OECD, 2019[80]). While over 80% of individuals in OECD countries use the Internet to exchange e-mails, less than 60% do so to get information from or interact with government services, and only half of the population buys goods or services online (ITU, 2021[97]). This gap is considerably wider in Georgia, where the uptake of digital tools remains below OECD and EU levels (Figure 2.2). E-commerce, for instance, is not yet as widespread: less than one third of the Georgian population seeks information about goods and services on the Internet and only 14% shop online. Some

---

[6] The baseline corresponds to the median value for Sundays between 3 January and 6 February 2020 for the use of public transport, and for Mondays of the same period for visits to workplace.

estimates suggest that e-commerce represents as little as 1.1% of total retail sales in Georgia in 2020, against 12% in Europe (Galt & Taggart, 2021[95]). However, local online marketplaces, such as Mymarket.ge and Extra.ge, are currently experiencing strong user growth.

Figure 2.2. Internet activities undertaken by individuals in the EaP, OECD and EU-8 countries

Percentage of population, 2018 or latest year available

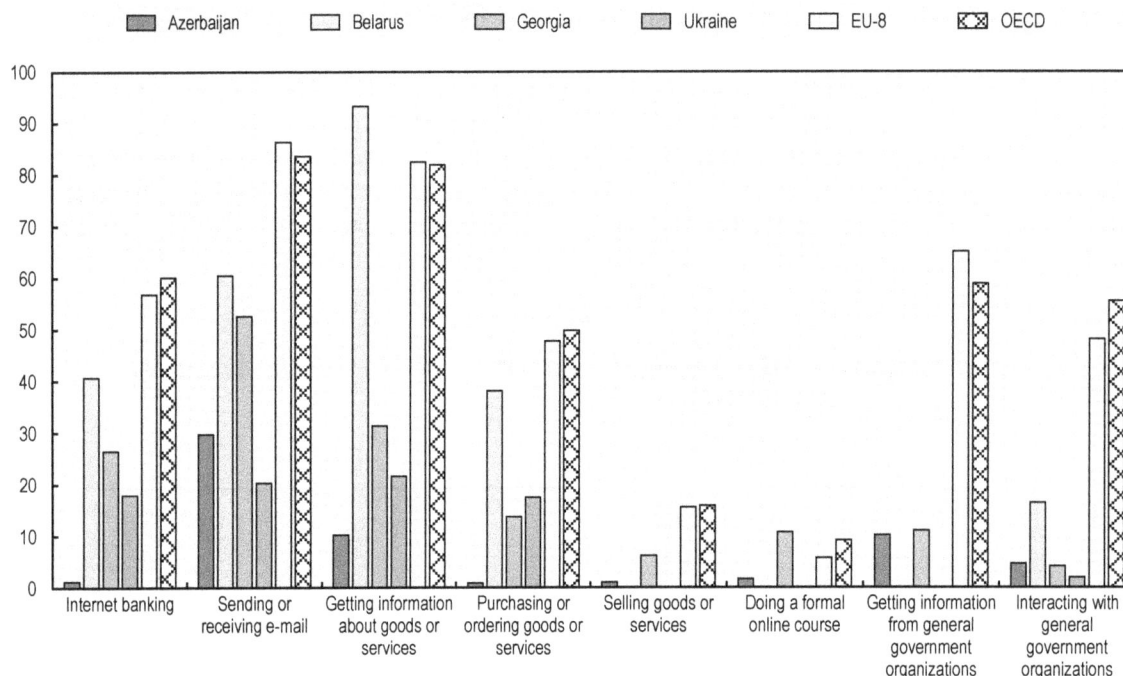

Note: Median values for OECD and EU-8. Data not available for Armenia and Moldova. Data on selling goods or services, doing a formal online course and getting information from general government organisations not available for Belarus and Ukraine.
Source: (ITU, 2021[97]).

Similar gaps in technology uptake appear with regard to businesses. Despite good connectivity (94% of Georgian companies had access to the Internet in 2020), most of them are not using basic digital technologies such as enterprise resource planning or e-booking and orders systems (Figure 2.3).

Moreover, despite the presence of some high-tech companies in Georgia, the majority of traditional businesses have not yet adopted advanced technologies. Only few Georgian companies offering AI services for traditional businesses have emerged: the fintech start-up *Optio.AI*, for example, enables financial firms to categorise their customers' transactions and provides tailored advice on spend optimisation through an AI-powered Chabot. The firm has recently partnered with the Bank of Georgia to develop a Virtual Assistant (Optio.AI, 2021[98]).

As for blockchain technology, although its uptake remains low among traditional companies, Georgia is home to the largest cryptocurrency mining company in the world, Bitfury (World Bank Group, 2018[99]). This company controls 10-15% of global cryptocurenncy mining, and, as a result, it has expanded across the world through the construction of new facilities in a number of countries. Due to its success in the field, the company is now a partner of the Georgian National Blockchain Agency (GNBA), with aims at accelerating the adoption of this technology in the country (Georgian National Blockchain Agency, 2018[100]). Finally, although IoT can increase the efficiency of supply chain and logistics management, its adoption by Georgian businesses is still at a nascent stage. However, a few international companies, like the French-based company Prodware, provide support to adopt IT solutions aimed at improving production processes in the country.

The gaps in technology adoption are more evident when diffusion rates are analysed by enterprise size classes. Despite the lack of size-disaggregated data for Georgia, statistical evidence from other countries suggests that this tendency affects all countries, with relative gaps between large and small firms becoming more evident as technologies are more advanced (Figure 2.3). Large firms are twice as likely to adopt online tools to receive and process orders than smaller ones but about four times more likely to use emerging technologies such as big data analytics or AI.

Figure 2.3. Diffusion rates of digital technologies, by technology and enterprise size class

Percentage of enterprises using the technology, 2020 or latest available

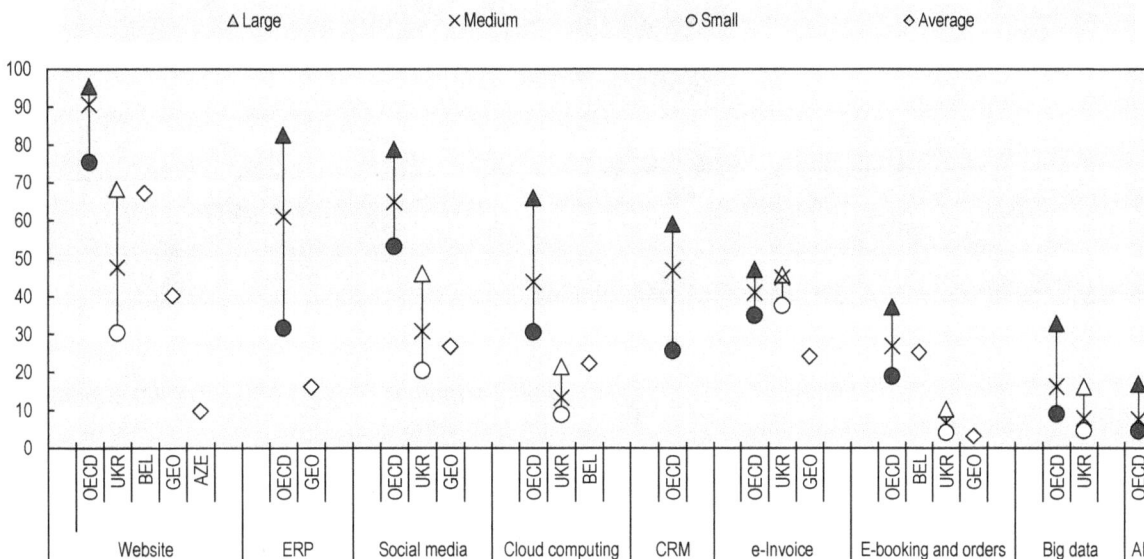

Note: Median value for OECD. Data does not include enterprises with less than 10 employees, as small enterprises refer to firms with 10 to 49 employees.
Source: OECD ICT Access and Usage by Businesses Database, National Statistical Authorities of Azerbaijan, Belarus, Georgia and Ukraine. Data for Armenia and Moldova not available. Adapted from (OECD, 2021[89]).

These digital divides harm economic growth and risk increasing inequalities, as SMEs' delay in digitalisation prevents them from reaping the productivity gains offered by the adoption of digital tools, thereby widening the existing productivity gap.

Policymakers have a key role to play to support the digital transformation

While the COVID-19 crisis has incentivised firms to accelerate their digital transformation, policymakers have a major role to play to facilitate this transition through complementary policy interventions. Building a truly digital economy and society will require a comprehensive cross-governmental approach to ensure access to high-quality and affordable broadband connection, to create an enabling regulatory environment for the development of digital practices while also ensuring users' security and trust, as well as to develop high levels of digital literacy. These efforts need to be complemented by tools to support SME digitalisation in particular.

In this regard, policymakers should level the playing field between small and large firms by addressing the factors that hinder the former and benefit the latter. This requires a two-fold framework aimed at a successful digital transformation of SMEs that includes stimulating technology adoption while concurrently promoting digital culture diffusion (Figure 2.4).

Figure 2.4. Framework for supporting the digital transformation of SMEs in the EaP

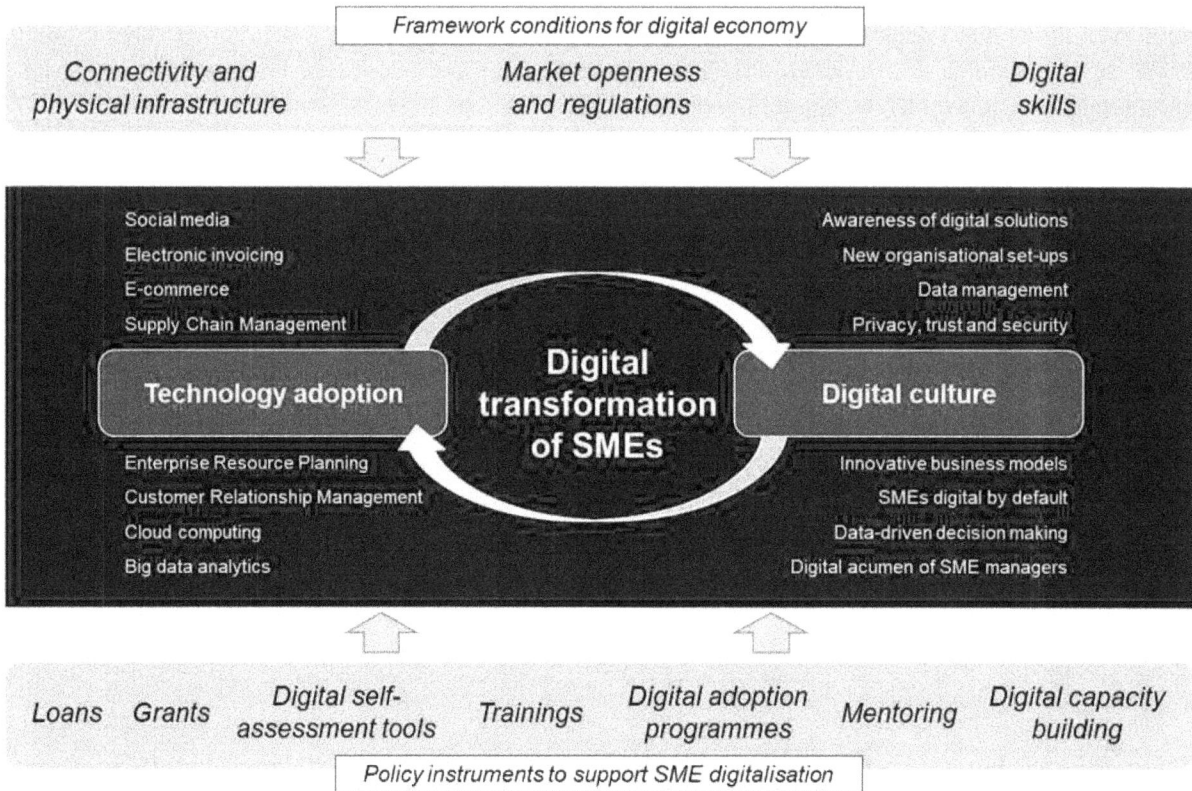

Source: OECD analysis.

Georgia has been developing the institutional and policy framework to support digitalisation over the past decade. It was one of the first Eastern Partner countries to adopt a dedicated strategy, *A Digital Georgia: e-Georgia Strategy and Action Plan 2014-2018*. Organised around 11 thematic pillars, the document aimed at setting a framework for ICT use and developing e-government, while fostering digital innovation in the business sector and the civil society. Regarding digital government, the strategy became part of the *Public Administration Reform 2020*, the policy roadmap adopted in 2015 to enhance the efficiency, effectiveness and transparency of the central public administration and its services, which included digital government as a priority. This policy framework enabled the operationalisation of an open data portal (data.gov.ge) and the further development of the unified portal of e-services (my.gov.ge), as well as awareness-raising campaigns to provide information and train civil servants and the public on the use of such services. Additional measures on digital government are currently being planned under a second National Digital Governance Strategy and Action Plan, drafted with the support of the UNDP and United Nations University experts.

As for the business sector, the previous e-Georgia Strategy focused on facilitating business transactions by encouraging the uptake of digital tools, such as online payments, setting standards of security and transparency, and improving broadband infrastructure. For example, the National Bank of Georgia introduced in 2017 a regulation to protect customers' rights and ensure transparency, by registering payment service providers and by introducing the obligation to respond to complaints (National Bank of

Georgia, 2017[101]). Moreover, e-commerce regulations have been strengthened to include data protection, and access to broadband infrastructures has been widened (see below for more detail).

More recently, within the framework of the EU4Digital programme and with the support of the European Commission and the World Bank Group, Georgia elaborated the *National Broadband Development Strategy of Georgia* (NBDS) and its Action Plan for 2020-2025, which was adopted by the Government of Georgia on 10 January 2020. The key objectives of this umbrella document are to enhance the legal and regulatory framework for broadband development in line with the EU norms and to overcome the digital divide across urban and rural areas. The targets of the NBDS are based on the EU's Gigabit Society objectives 2025. The NBDS foresees work on three main directions: 1) increase competitive pressure; 2) attract investments; and 3) build digital skills & demand. For the implementation of these directions, the Government of Georgia together with the World Bank started the *Log-in Georgia Project*, aimed at increasing access to affordable broadband Internet, promoting the use of broadband-enabled digital services, and providing project implementation support.

Additional policy measures related to the digital transformation are included in cross-cutting policy documents such as the new SME Development Strategy 2021-2025 and related action plans, and the government programme for 2021-2024 "Toward Building a European State", which encompasses a chapter dedicated to ICT. The COVID-19 pandemic also incentivised the Georgian authorities to take additional ad-hoc measures in response to the crisis (see Box 2.2). The solutions adopted have further encouraged the diffusion of digital tools across the Georgian society and fostered the digitalisation of public services, while showing the authorities' ability to react in a quick and innovative way.

Georgia is currently developing a *Long-term National Strategy for the development of the digital economy and information society* and its implementation plan. The goal of this umbrella document, drafted by a working group under the Ministry of Economy and Sustainable Development with the help of the World Bank, will be to foster economic development through the expansion of e-government services, the use of digital technologies to boost sustainable development, the promotion of digital literacy and skills to foster job creation, and the promotion of fintech, e-Trade, eHealth, cybersecurity, ICT innovations, and the fourth industrial revolution, including through AI.

Box 2.2. Examples of digital solutions adopted by Georgian authorities in response to COVID-19

Ad hoc digital tools

Communication and notification operations centre

A communication and operation centre was established and supervised by the order of the MoESD. This Operations centre, which included representatives of the Ministry, of the Communications Commission (ComCom) and of the telecommunication and postal companies, aimed at strengthening co-operation and coordination, so that companies could respond immediately to damages and delays in telecommunication and postal courier services due to the increased demand.

"Stop Covid" mobile application for iOS and Android

The Ministry of Health created this mobile application as a platform that allowed to trace the spread of the infection and to give relevant information to the population.

Other mobile tools

A number of hotlines (e.g. 112, 144, 114) were introduced to provide information and guidance on different issues related to the COVID-19 crisis, e.g. to obtain a one-time movement permit. SMS were also used to provide updated information, including a version in minority languages and a formal communication channel in Georgian and English was created on the social media platform "Telegram".

Increase in the provision of online services

Online clinics were developed in order to provide virtual medical consultations, and reduce doctors' visits. This instrument helped monitoring cases, as it allowed reaching a larger amount of individuals.

Distance learning was introduced, as well as a number of digital tools to support it. The Georgian Government together with the Public Broadcaster launched the "TV School", which broadcasted lessons from the national curriculum. A "Webschool" project promoted by the Ministry of Education offered webinars to final year students to prepare them for exams. Access to pupils' profiles, without the intermediary work of the school administration, was provided through a portal created *ad hoc*. Teachers were also supported in the transition to online schooling through virtual consultation spaces where IT experts provided assistance, as part of the "New School model".

Legal services have been adapted to an online format, e.g. court trials and meetings of the Standing Commission (that decides over conditional sentences and lifting of conviction) took place online.

Additional e-government services were introduced to my.gov.ge, e.g. all business registry services, as well as reservation to visit Public Service halls, Community Centres and several public agencies. Pensions and allowances were set or renewed electronically by sending a document copy by email.

Tighter co-operation between the government, regulator and telecom operators

Wholesale broadband service providers were able to double their international data capacity to ensure that the increased demand would not affect the provision of the service.

An **agreement with mobile operators** allowed to distribute free sim cards at Georgian airports in order to provide access to the "Stop Covid" application and "112" hotline. Free Wi-Fi hotspots were equipped to show pop-up information upon passengers' connection.

Source: (Government of Georgia, 2020[102]), (EU4Digital, 2020[103]), (Lomsadze, 2021[104]) and (OECD, 2021[96]).

The main stakeholders designing and implementing digitalisation policies in Georgia are the MoESD and the Digital Governance Agency (DGA). The MoESD, through the Communications, Information and Modern Technologies Department, acts as the main policymaker in the digital field and implements different reforms, projects, programmes and activities with other stakeholders to improve the accessibility of broadband Internet and ICT technologies for individuals and businesses, including SMEs. The Digital Governance Agency was created in 2020 as a result of the merger between the former Data Exchange Agency and Smart Logic, an LEPL under the Ministry of Justice of Georgia that used to provide services for a number of Ministries, Departments and Agencies. The DGA operates under the Ministry of Justice of Georgia, and it is responsible for the digital transformation of public services and interagency co-ordination, notably creating a unified data exchange system, preparing draft legislation on digital governance and cybersecurity, and fostering regional and international co-operation. The Ministry of Education and Science is also involved on digital literacy policies at all stages of the education system and through vocational education. With regard to small and medium businesses, the bulk of support to SME digitalisation is currently provided by GITA, while Enterprise Georgia offers assistance on e-commerce, such as co-financing of fees to place products on digital marketplaces (Figure 2.5).

Figure 2.5. Institutional framework for digitalisation in Georgia

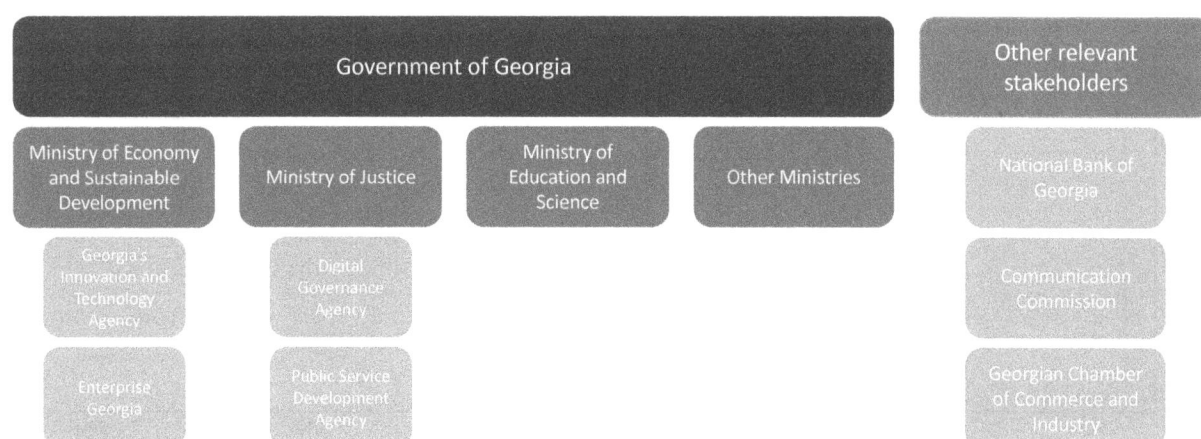

Source: OECD authors based on fact-finding questionnaires, working group meetings and desk research.

Building an enabling environment

Improving broadband connectivity

Reliable connectivity is a pre-requisite for the development of digital economies and societies. Internet access has become more and more important for individuals and businesses alike, as they increase and diversify their online activities – from getting information and sending emails to Internet banking and e-commerce. It is also fundamental for the digital transformation of businesses: an increase of 10 percentage points in the adoption of high-speed Internet among firms can improve productivity by 0.8 to 1.9% (Sorbe et al., 2019[105]). Broadband connectivity can benefit even smaller firms, for instance by enabling them to enlarge their customer/market base and/or increase operational efficiency by giving them access to cost-effective solutions (e.g. CRM, ERP, payment solutions), although SMEs operating in traditional sectors often lack awareness of them. The necessity of ensuring a high-speed and affordable connection throughout territories has been further highlighted by the COVID-19 crisis: following the introduction of social distancing measures, remote work and education, the demand for broadband soared, increasing by up to 60% during the first wave of infections in Spring 2020 (OECD, 2020[106]). While this unprecedented surge put a considerable pressure on communication networks and operators, it also revealed persisting digital divides between individuals and firms – e.g, between age groups, with individuals aged 55-74 lagging behind the 16-24 year old population, and between education levels (less than half the OECD adult population with low or no formal education used the Internet to interact with government authorities in 2018, against 80% of those with tertiary education) (OECD, 2020[107]). There is also remaining gaps between urban and rural areas, and between large and small businesses, as further explained below.

Overall, Georgia appears as one of the most connected countries in the Eastern Partnership, with fixed and mobile subscriptions per 100 inhabitants reaching 24 and 80 in 2019, respectively (Figure 2.6, Figure 2.7). These numbers have seen the sharpest increase of the region since 2010 (+429% against +207% in the EaP and +36% in OECD for fixed broadband, and +1011% for mobile broadband, against 938% in the EaP and 216% in the OECD).

Figure 2.6. Evolution of fixed broadband subscriptions in Georgia compared to EaP, EU and OECD

Fixed broadband subscriptions per 100 inhabitants, 2010-2019

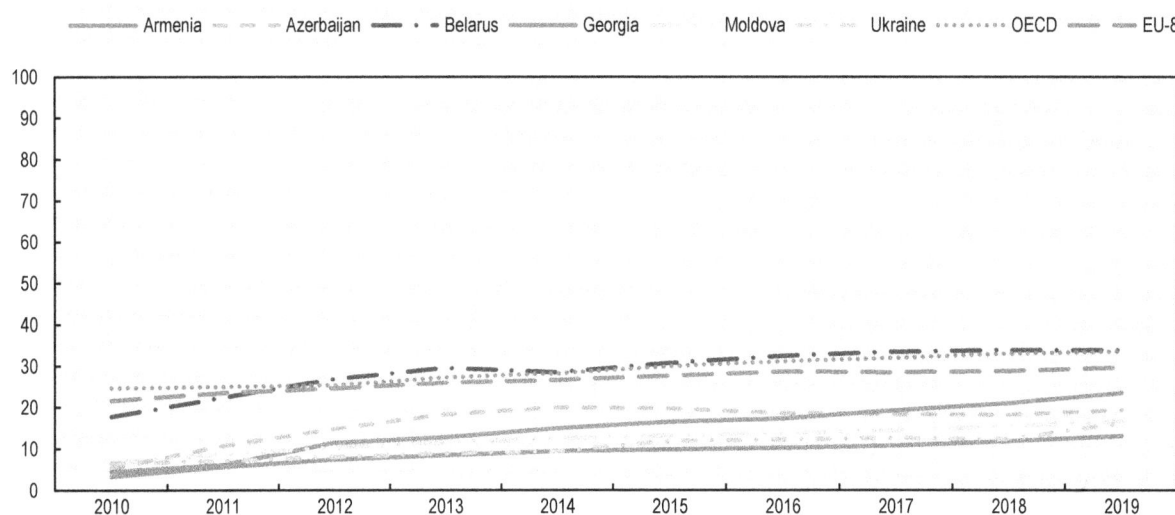

Note: Median values for OECD and EU-8 (Czech Republic, Estonia, Hungary, Latvia, Lithuania, Slovenia, Slovak Republic, Poland).
Source: (ITU, 2021[108]).

Figure 2.7. Evolution of mobile broadband subscriptions in Georgia compared to EaP, EU and OECD

Mobile broadband subscriptions per 100 inhabitants, 2010-2019

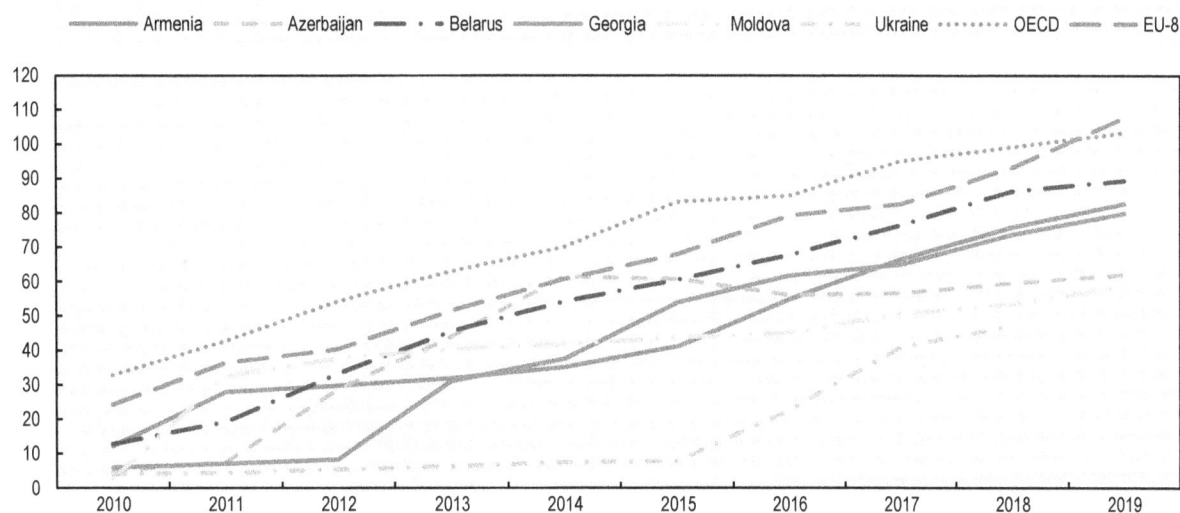

Note: Median values for OECD and EU-8 (Czech Republic, Estonia, Hungary, Latvia, Lithuania, Slovenia, Slovak Republic, Poland). Data for 2019 not available for Ukraine.
Source: (ITU, 2021[108]).

Although 86% of Georgian households had access to the Internet at home in 2020, data show persistent disparities across space. Rural areas still lag behind, with a 16-percentage point gap between them and the urban parts of the country. However, this difference has shrunk over the past years, and is now lower than that of most EaP countries, albeit well above OECD and EU figures (Figure 2.8, Figure 2.9) .The Georgian authorities are well aware of this connectivity challenge and have put the issue at the top of the digitalisation agenda. Some mountainous regions such as Tusheti, Pshav-Khevsurebi and Gudamakari have benefitted from the development of community networks, i.e. community-deployed communications infrastructures resulting from public-private partnerships involving the local community, local and central governments, the MoESD, ComCom (formerly GNCC), private businesses, the European Bureau of Internet Society (ISOC), and international donors. These provided Internet connection to two ravines and 24 villages in mountainous Tusheti in 2017, and to up to 100 villages (i.e. about 500 families) in Pshav-Khevsurebi and Gudamakari valleys in 2020. They also fostered the local economy through tourism and agriculture: as an example, equipping local hotels and guesthouses in these mountainous areas with a reliable connection helps attract more demand from local and international hikers (Small and Medium Telecom Operators Association of Georgia and Tusheti Development Fund, 2018[109]). Further policy efforts are planned, as the government aims to continue supporting the deployment of community networks in less-densely populated areas. Adjara notably should benefit from these.

Figure 2.8. Rural digital divide in EaP countries　　Figure 2.9 Rural digital divide in Georgia, 2012-2019

% of households with Internet access at home, 2019 or latest year available　　% of households with Internet access at home

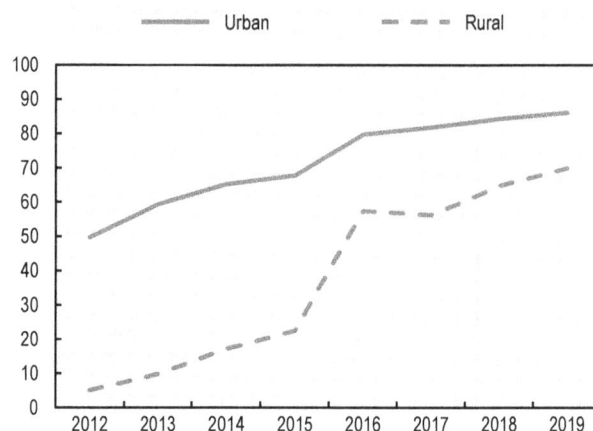

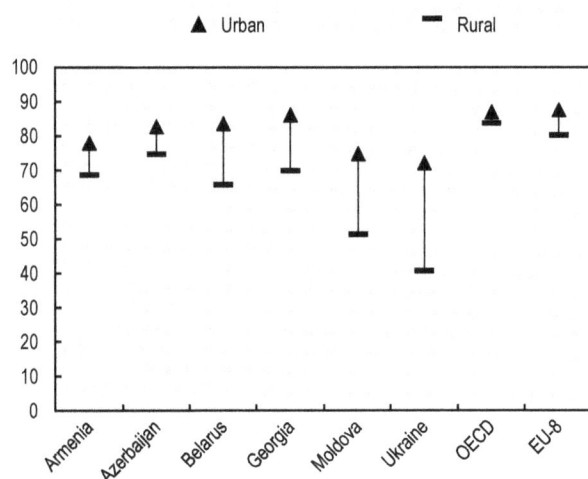

Note: Data refer to 2019 except for Armenia (2016) and Ukraine (2018).　　Source: (ITU, 2021[108]).
Median values for OECD and EU-8.
Source: (ITU, 2021[108]).

Access to broadband alone is however not sufficient to bridge the connectivity gap: the digital transformation requires ensuring high-quality connection at affordable prices. The quality of the Internet connection in Georgia has improved over the past years: 3G/4G mobile networks now cover the majority of the Georgian territory, and 85% of fixed broadband subscriptions offer a speed beyond 10 Mbps. However, many Georgian businesses do not yet benefit from quality Internet connection: while the vast majority have access to the Internet (94%), 41% still have a connection below 10 Mbps. Moving forward, the new NBDS 2020-2025 aims at ensuring a 99% 4G coverage and the introduction of pilots for 5G services in three municipalities by 2025; that all households have access to high-speed Internet (at least 100 Mbps); and 1 Gbps for all institutional entities. Georgia is also working on 5G deployment, notably through large-scale works on developing infrastructure (ITU, 2020[110]). In addition, the ComCom has worked on spectrum availability, reserve price calculation and license obligations, and an auction should be held in 2021 to issue the frequency spectrum required, although it has not yet been announced. The country is also co-operating with neighbouring countries to coordinate frequencies: the ComCom reported having reached agreements with EaP countries on the topic, which should minimise incoming signals from them and help preventing radio interferences between communication networks, thereby ensuring their proper functioning.

The gap in uptake between fixed and mobile broadband can be partially explained by the differences in affordability. While prices for mobile connection in Georgia are among the lowest in the EaP region when expressed as percentage of monthly gross national income per capita, fixed broadband still appear quite costly, as they remain above ITU's 2% affordability target (Figure 2.10, Figure 2.11). Yet businesses need strong and reliable broadband connections, as their activities can be bandwidth heavy – fixed broadband often offers better speed, e.g. for uploading/downloading content or running software. Reducing costs for fixed broadband would therefore help improve firms' connectivity and foster their uptake of digital tools. However, the NBDS does not foresee business-specific measures, but rather focuses economically disadvantaged groups, for which subsidies to access the Internet are planned.

Figure 2.10. ICT prices – fixed broadband

% GNI per capita

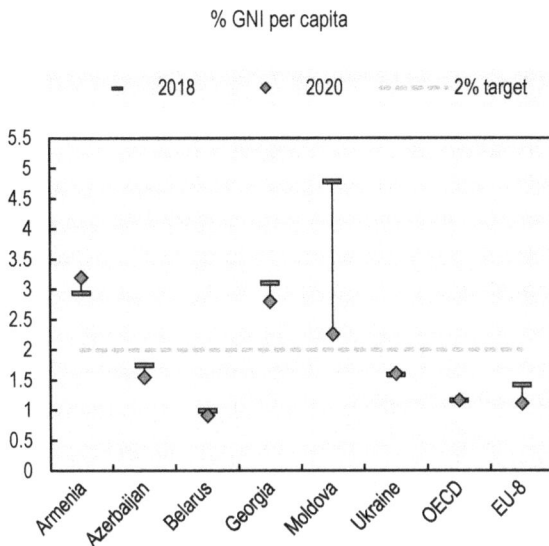

Note: GNI = gross national income. Prices refer to a fixed-broadband basket with a monthly data usage of (a minimum of) 5 GB. Median values for OECD and EU-8.
Source: (ITU, 2021[108]).

Figure 2.11. ICT prices – mobile broadband

% GNI per capita

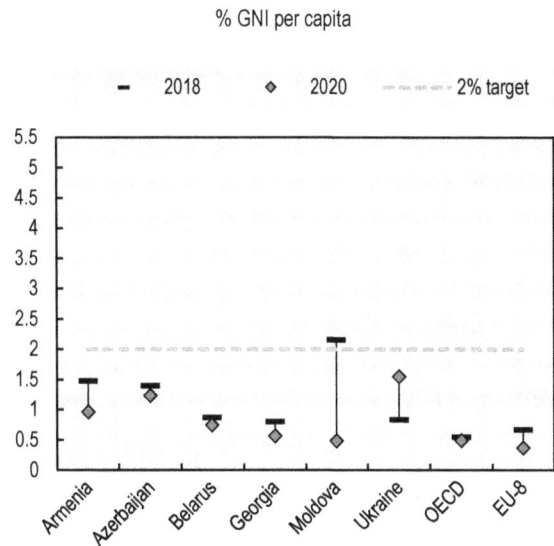

Note: GNI = gross national income. Prices refer to a data-only mobile broadband basket with a monthly data allowance of 1.5 GB. Median values for OECD and EU-8.
Source: (ITU, 2021[108]).

Affordable access to high-speed broadband can be increased by policy and regulatory measures, such as promoting competition to attract investment in communications infrastructures and services (OECD, 2019[80]). Georgia's new NBDS defines it as a priority, and the country has already taken some steps in that direction. The Law on Electronic Communications was amended to increase market regulation and address the current oligopoly, as the ComCom reported that a few operators gather significant market power and reportedly try to ignore legal requirements (Communication Commission, 2021[111]). The new provisions grant more power to the ComCom, allowing for more effective enforcement mechanisms in case of non-compliance, including sanctions in case of violation of the tariff regulation. The new regulation also enables ComCom to appoint more easily a special manager to enforce state decisions instead of revoking the authorisation of the non-compliant company, which ultimately aims at ensuring the services' stability and thereby at safeguarding consumers. Foreign direct investments can also play an important role in fostering infrastructure development and strengthening competition. In the OECD *FDI Restrictiveness Index*, Georgia scores high among EaP countries, having no formal barriers to foreign direct investment in the telecommunication sector, with conditions that could be compared to the most open OECD economies (OECD, 2019[112]). As the Index considers only formal barriers, informal barriers, e.g. corruption, could still reduce competition and should not be overlooked.

Georgia could build on its existing good quality infrastructure and encourage infrastructure sharing by adopting the draft law on Sharing Telecommunication Infrastructure and Physical Infrastructure Used for Telecommunication Purposes. This regulation would enable operators to make use of the existing infrastructure on non-discriminatory and competitive terms, allowing for more market competition and optimised hence reduced costs for network providers. In turn, this should incentivise them to offer higher quality services at lower prices.

Finally, Georgia is involved in several regional and international initiatives aimed at improving broadband telecommunication infrastructure, speed and affordability. The country has the ambition to become a digital hub for the South Caucasus. To that end, negotiations between the MoESD and foreign telecommunications operators are underway to encourage them to enter Georgia, as well as to establish data centres on the national territory. The establishment of a digital telecommunications corridor that would provide a modern transit fibre optic infrastructure network connecting Europe to Asia via Georgia, Armenia and Azerbaijan is also being discussed. At the Eastern Partnership level, the six countries have been working towards the harmonisation of their regulatory frameworks and prices with the support of the EU4Digital initiative, which should improve interoperability and reduce charges. A Regional Roaming Agreement has been negotiated to harmonise the international mobile roaming regulatory framework and costs among them. It should enter into force on 1 July 2022 and is expected to lead to an 87% decrease in roaming prices by 2026 (EU4Digital, 2021[113]). EU4Digital is studying options for a similar agreement between EaP countries and the EU.

Creating a regulatory framework for the digital transformation

Georgia has been developing a legal and regulatory framework in the field of ICT in line with EU standards (EU4Digital, 2020[114]), which is reflected by its good performance in the indicators of the World Economic Forum's Network Readiness Index 2020. Georgia's ICT regulatory framework ranks 21st out of 134 countries, and its regulatory quality 24th (World Economic Forum, 2020[115]). The country benefits from a national regulatory authority (NRA), the above-mentioned ComCom, whose institutional and financial independence is guaranteed by Georgia's Constitution since 2017. A recent independent assessment also found the authority's activities to be transparent and matching EU requirements in many regards – e.g. its decisions can be appealed and are subject to a fair judicial process (EU4Digital, 2020[114]).

However, in order to align further with EU regulations, any budget surplus should be transferred to market participants (instead of being sent to the State Budget, as it is currently the case). Overall, the harmonisation of ICT regulation is facilitated by the regional co-operation: Georgia regularly exchanges with other EaP countries and the EU on these topics through the EaPeReg network and expert groups, to which the ComCom participates as an active member. This platform gathers NRAs from EaP countries and provides them with a platform for co-operation on regulatory matters related to electronic communications. Further enhancing the legal and regulatory environment also appears as a key objective of the NBDS.

E-commerce and consumer protection

E-commerce practices have been growing in Georgia, with a sharp increase prompted by the COVID-19 crisis. The size of the Georgian e-commerce market more than tripled in 2020, reaching GEL 138 million (approx. USD 44 million) (Galt & Taggart, 2021[95]). Many firms have been forced to move their activities online due to lockdowns and social distancing. As for the demand side, the share of Georgians above 15 years of age using the Internet to shop online increased by 15% between 2016 and 2020 (+50% among 15-29 year-olds) (Geostat, 2021[116]). However, there is still huge potential for growth, as e-commerce accounted for only 1.1% of total retail sales in 2020, and OECD estimates show that the e-commerce market in Georgia is one of the smallest of the EaP region in absolute terms (Statista, 2021[117]). In that regard, enhancing the legal and regulatory framework for e-commerce practices would help tap into the potential of online trade: on the one hand, harmonisation with EU directives would facilitate access to the EU market. On the other hand, legal tools can foster consumers' trust by ensuring their protection online.

E-commerce legislation is Georgia's lowest ranked indicator in the Network Readiness Index (World Economic Forum, 2020[115]) (115th out of 134 countries). Indeed, the country still lacks a legal framework regulating e-trade practices, which is required by the Association Agreement with the EU. Online platform regulation and consumer protection are incompletely covered by fragmented acts of legislation. In order to tackle this issue, the MoESD has elaborated a draft law on e-Commerce in 2018, which should align with the EU e-commerce directive and DCFTA requirements. This new legislation should define the rights and obligations of operators of intermediary service providers, and strengthen consumers' protection, increasing reliability for SMEs as well as costumers.

Another draft law, dedicated to Consumer Rights, should provide further guarantees by setting requirements against aggressive commercial practices, standardise contracts between parties transacting online, and ensure that the consumer receives all relevant information (EU4Digital, 2021[118]). In general, legal harmonisation is fostered by Georgia's active participation in the EU4Digital programme, where the MoESD acts as national co-ordinator, to facilitate EaP countries' access to the EU's Digital Single Market.

However, some obstacles to e-commerce with the EU are not yet covered by any of the draft laws. There is for instance a lack of interoperability of parcel-delivery operations due to the absence of national standards in tracking, tracing and labelling parcels. On a similar note, the legislation does not define whether a contract is ruled by the law of the consumer's country of residence. Georgia is also not in line with several provisions of the new EU 2021 e-commerce package, e.g. regarding customs declaration, fiscal regulations, and cross-border parcels' supply chain practices. Moreover, there is a lack of awareness of the upcoming EU changes in VAT payments, customs procedures, and electronic declarations, which prevents stakeholders to start preparatory actions.

E-signatures

E-signatures can take a variety of forms, ranging from a simple photocopy of a physical signature to different levels of verified signature. They are important in ensuring that a document respects integrity requirements while avoiding physical paperwork, and can provide in many cases proof of one's identity. Due to e-signatures' legal value and the variety of forms they can take, a legal framework that regulates their use is essential to guarantee reliability and thereby strengthen interaction transparency and security, and increase users' trust.

With this aim, the parliament introduced as early as 2008 a *Law on Electronic Document and Digital Signature* (Government of Georgia, 2008[119]), which defines how to request the certification of electronic signature and the requirements to issue such a certification. The legislation was profoundly updated following Georgia's e-Strategy 2014-2018. Indeed, the action plan highlighted the importance of promoting the use of e-signatures, as they can ensure increased security in online interactions such as e-commerce transactions and procedures involving public authorities. As a result, in 2017 the *Law on Electronic Document and Electronic Trusted Services* granted legal status to electronic signatures and documents (Government of Georgia, 2017[120]). These modifications made it possible to receive a number of legal services remotely, advancing Georgian e-governance, and envisaged that any entity meeting the requirements outlined by the law can become a qualified trust provider. As a result, this service is not anymore carried out only by the governmental body LEPL Public Service Development Agency (SDA), as happened until 2018, but can be offered by a variety of bodies. The use of e-signatures was further encouraged since 2019 by obliging any company that conducts business with administrative bodies to sign documents using a recognised electronic signature or stamp (EU4Digital, 2019[121]). Since 2020, the law has been subject to an update, which has not yet been finalised (Parliament of Georgia, 2020[122]).

Nowadays, Georgia enjoys, along with Ukraine and Moldova, one of the region's most complete legal frameworks for e-signatures. However, Georgia, unlike Ukraine and Moldova, has not yet harmonised its legislation with the EU electronic IDentification And Trust Services (eIDAS) regulation and recommendations. The diversity of electronic identity (eID) and eSignature systems across the EaP countries hinders cross-border exchanges (EU4Digital, 2020[123]). In order to overcome this issue, EU4Digital Facility has launched the eSignature pilot initiative, which consists in the recognition of cross-border eSignature between Ukraine and Moldova (EaP-EaP), and Ukraine and Estonia (EaP-EU). The aim is to analyse the technical as well as the organisational aspects of this mutual recognition process, in order to extend the Digital Single Market to the other EaP countries, including Georgia.

Digital security, data privacy and protection to enhance trust

Building trust in the digital economy is a pre-condition for the digital transformation. As individuals, governments and businesses rapidly increase their online activities, they face ever-growing digital security threats such as phishing campaigns, malwares or cybersquatting. These can cause significant economic and social losses, from disruption of operations to damages to reputation and competitiveness, leading to financial losses. They particularly affect SMEs, who often lack awareness of the risks and resources to counter them (OECD, 2016[124]). Georgia has developed a policy and legal framework to address this issue, which has positioned it among leaders in the EaP region in international rankings such as ITU's Global Cybersecurity Index (GCI) 2020 (Figure 2.12) and the National Cybersecurity Index 2020.

Figure 2.12. Georgia's scores in the Global Cybersecurity Index 2020, per pillar

Scale from 0 to 20

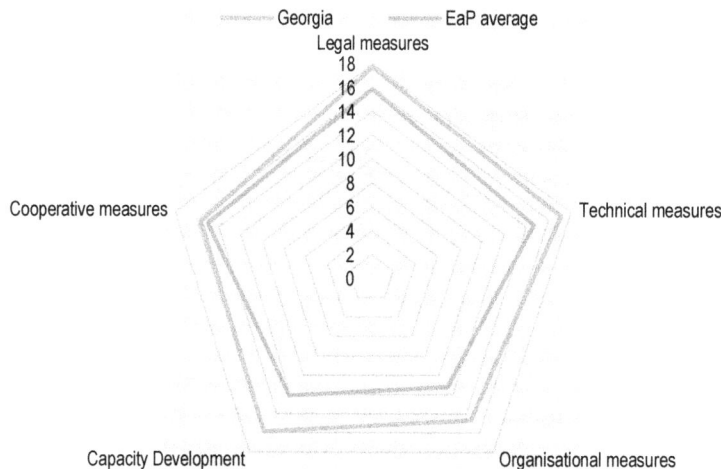

Note: **Legal measures** refer to the presence of legislations, regulations and other rules related to digital security; **Technical measures** to the existence of technical institutions and framework for digital security; **Organisational measures** to the presence of coordination institutions, policies and strategies at the national level; **Capacity Development** to research and development, education and training programmes, certified professionals and capacity building, and **Cooperative measures** to partnerships, cooperative frameworks and information sharing networks. Source: (ITU, 2021[125]).

Georgia is one of the few EaP countries to have adopted a dedicated strategy and action plans on digital security issues. It enacted its first Cybersecurity Strategy as early as 2012 (Government of Georgia, 2012[126]), followed by a second one in 2017. Both documents focused on researching these issues for evidence-based policymaking, enacting a legal and regulatory framework, defining stakeholders' responsibilities and coordination mechanisms, raising awareness and fostering international co-operation (United Nations, 2019[127]). The DGA elaborated a third National Cybersecurity Strategy and Action Plan for 2021-2024, which has been enacted by the Government of Georgia in September 2021 (Government of Georgia, 2021[128]). This new document is expected to strengthen the resilience of both the public and private sector by developing a culture among society and organisations of cybersecurity risks and the skills to enact mitigating measures, bolstering the governance systemic-operation, and enhancing Georgia's participation in international co-operation initiatives.

Georgia has also built a dedicated institutional framework, composed of stakeholders responsible for designing and implementing digital security policies: the DGA (formerly Data Exchange Agency until 2020), the State Security Service of Georgia, the Cyber Security Bureau of the Ministry of Defence, and the National Bank of Georgia. With regard to the legislation in place, Georgia adopted in 2012 a *Law on Information Security*, which provides an initial legal framework, refining roles and notably creating the above-mentioned Cyber Security Bureau. As of June 2020, EU4Digital reported that the Georgian legislation is still not in line with the EU's Directive on Security of Network and Information Systems (NIS directive), but the law was amended in June 2021 to strengthen the framework (Parliament of Georgia, 2021[129]).

Moreover, building "incident response capabilities" is necessary to help public and private organisations manage risks and improve resilience (OECD, 2015[130]). Such systems enable firms and administrations to report cyber incidents – and thereby centralise and monitor them – design adequate responses to tackle them, raise awareness of potential threats, and foster national and international co-operation. Georgia has established three computer emergency response teams (CERT) so far – cert.gov.ge, created in 2011, operating under the DGA, the Cyber Security Bureau (for the Ministry of Defence) and the academic CERT GRENA (Georgian Research and Educational Networking Association). However, they could be improved: the cert.gov.ge website is not yet user-friendly and often suffers from disruptions, and the resources made available online are very limited. Georgia also lacks funding and expertise on digital security issues (EU4Digital, 2020[131]). Moreover, private firms are not, as in some European countries such as Austria, legally obliged to meet any minimum cybersecurity requirements or to report cybersecurity incidents – such legal obligations only apply to operators of critical infrastructure, which reduces the response and monitoring capacity.

At the individual and firm levels, Georgians have benefitted from several initiatives aimed at raising their awareness of cybersecurity threats and developing their skills. GITA's IT training for instance include a cybersecurity component (GITA, 2021[132]). Cyber Olympiads are organised by the CERT of the DGA since 2016, where cybersecurity students can improve their knowledge and skills by trying to solve real-case scenarios. Georgia could consider taking part in similar exercises at the regional and/or international level, akin to the European Cyber Security Challenge (https://ecsc.eu/) powered by the European Agency for Cybersecurity. Such competitions would also allow for benchmarking against peer countries.

Finally, Georgia is co-operating with international partners, such as the EU through the EU twinning project, the Council of Europe (CyberEast), the OSCE (e.g. Confidence Building Measures), and NATO. Georgia is also involved in the regional initiative GUAM (Organisation for Democracy and Economic Development) together with Azerbaijan, Moldova and Ukraine. The country also signed a memorandum of understanding on 5G security with the United States in January 2021.

Protecting personal data is another major aspect of digital security policies. Due to the steady rise in online activities and transactions, users' personal data are being increasingly collected by digital services providers, which expose them to potential breaches and personal data leaks. The law of Georgia on Personal Data Protection, adopted in 2011, aims at protecting users from these risks by setting some security requirements and rules for data processing, as well as obligations to data controllers and processors. In addition, the existence of a dedicated national supervisory authority, the State Inspector's Service, contributes to increasing online security. The authority controls the lawfulness of personal data processing activities in both the public and private sector, including e-commerce platforms. It inspected five private online platforms in 2020. It also issues recommendations on personal data processing for companies selling online.

Despite these achievements, the law on Personal Data Protection does not align with EU standards, such as the once-only principle (there is no legal requirements for data sharing and re-use), and the General

Data Protection Regulation (GDPR). A draft law on Personal Data Protection has been drafted and registered in the Parliament on 22 May 2019 to bring Georgian legislation closer to the GDPR, but has not yet entered into force.

Fostering digital skills development

Promoting digital skills is an essential component of the digital transformation: individuals and businesses cannot reap the benefits offered by new technologies without the ability to make use of them. Studies have shown that higher levels of digital literacy are positively correlated with higher employability and wages (OECD, 2015[133]). Conversely, skills shortages risk increasing the pre-existing divides between individuals, as those with higher digital proficiency levels can benefit from a wider range of online activities (training, shopping, e-government, etc.). That also applies to businesses, where the lack of digital skills among employees can limit the positive impact of digital technology on firms' profitability (Sorbe et al., 2019[105]).

Although Georgia benefits from high education levels and a skilled workforce, the country lags behind regional peers in terms of digital literacy (Figure 2.13). In 2019, only a third of the Georgian population had basic digital skills – against over half of the population in OECD and EU-8 countries. The share falls to 18% for standard skills such as basic usage of spreadsheet and presentation software, and to only 1% for individuals capable of writing a computer program using a specialised programming language.

Figure 2.13. ICT skills in EaP, OECD and EU-8 countries

By type of skills, 2019 or latest available

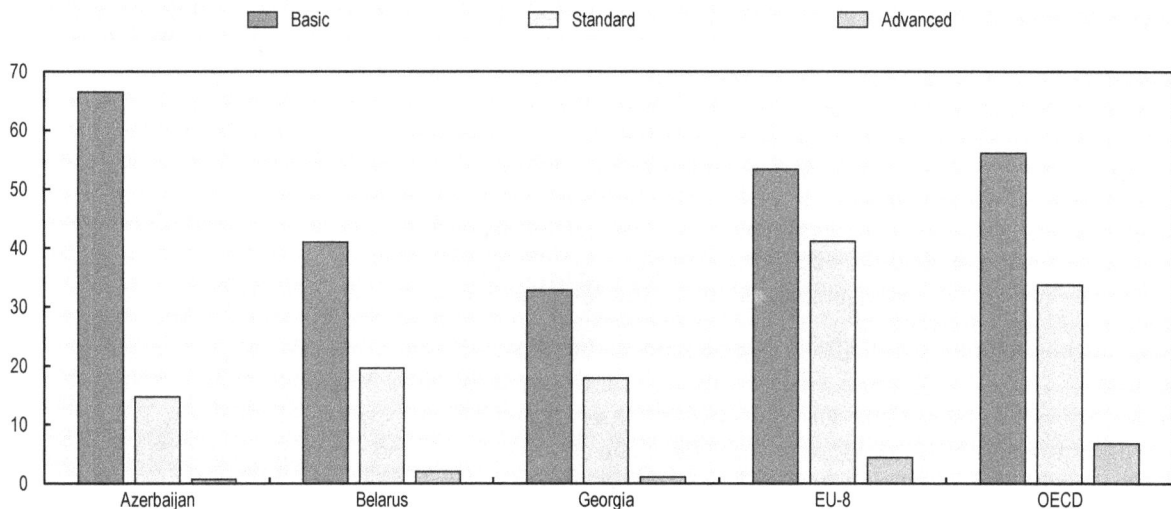

Note: Data not available for Armenia, Moldova and Ukraine. **Basic skills** correspond to copying or moving a file or folder, using copy and paste tools, sending e-mails with attached files, and transferring files between a computer and other devices; **standard skills** to using basic arithmetic formula in a spreadsheet; connecting and installing new devices; creating electronic presentations with presentation software; and finding, downloading, installing and configuring software; and **advanced** skills to writing a computer program using a specialised programming language. Source: (ITU, 2021[97]).

However, Georgia has made digital skills a public policy priority through various policy documents. The e-Georgia Strategy 2014-2018 already recognised the importance of digital skills (Krabina et al., 2017[134]), and the new NBDS set their promotion as one of its three key objectives. This political goal was also supported by Georgia's Unified Strategy for Education and Science 2017-2021, which defined the purpose of teaching ICT in schools and set the objective for all students to have a basic knowledge of ICT and practical experience in ICT usage upon completion of secondary education. To this end, and in order to facilitate teaching and learning, the New School Model introduced in 2018 foresees the implementation of digital technologies in teachers' working process (e.g. to make a schedule or communicate), and the effective use of electronic educational resources in the teaching and learning processes.

This impetus is supported by international partners such as the EU4Digital network[7]. As part of this, Georgia created an Action Plan to develop digital skills including measures to monitor and forecast national digital skills gaps to identify priority actions, and the creation of national coalitions for skills and jobs. The European Training Foundation is also helping with the promotion of digital competence in national curricula, and 15 VET institutions took part in one of its initiatives – the pilot of the Self-Assessment Tool SELFIE, an electronic questionnaire that assesses the uptake of digital technologies by educational institutions and allows Georgia to be compared to other countries such as France and Germany. The tool showed that VET institutions have a strong ICT base and use digital tools in teaching process. Lastly, the World Bank supports the use of digital tools in schools via its *Innovation, Inclusion and Quality* project.

The government has enacted several policy documents covering digital skills development. The NBDS plans, in co-operation with the Ministry of Education and Science, to support digital skills and literacy programmes, notably on digital security, focusing particularly on the youth. Additional measures are planned for people with disabilities and minorities. The Log-In Georgia Project has a component on training and capacity building programmes in regions to foster the uptake of e-services, from e-commerce to e-learning and e-government. The Unified Strategy of Education and Science 2022-2032 and the VET Strategy 2021-2025 are expected to further support the development of digital competencies among students and of remote learning.

Table 2.2. Selected policy initiatives to promote digital skills in Georgia

Policy direction	Policy achievements	Examples of planned measures moving forward
Promoting digital skills in primary and secondary education	Purpose of teaching ICT defined in the National Curriculum	
	Objective set for all students to have a basic knowledge of ICT and experience in ICT usage upon completion of general education institution	
	Digital competence defined as a key competence	
Fostering use of digital tools in education systems	Digital tools introduced in the working process of teachers (e.g. to make planning or communicate) & increased use of electronic educational resources in the teaching and learning process (New School Model)	Expansion of the New School Model to additional schools
	Schools provided with WiFi, laptops and projectors	
	COVID-19-induced distance learning: virtual classrooms created and Teleskola project with public broadcasting to develop television modes of distance learning	
	16 000 teachers trained in Distance teaching through Microsoft office	
	Microsoft office tools created to enable teachers to create e-resources themselves and exchange with peers	
	Microsoft Office user profiles created for up to 60 000 students and 55 000 teachers in public schools	

---

[7] EU4Digital is an EU initiative aiming to extend the EU's Digital Single Market to EaP countries and help them tap into the potential of digitalisation. For more information, see the dedicated website eufordigital.eu.

Policy direction	Policy achievements	Examples of planned measures moving forward
Promoting digital skills in higher education	Opening of the San Diego University Georgia offering internationally accredited STEM bachelor's degrees, with the financial support of the Millennium Challenge Corporation	Increase coordination between policymakers and academia
	Digital skills integrated into several higher education programmes	
	IT specialists' programme initiated by the GoG; GeoLab Junior programme launched by GITA in June 2021 to train students on online Front End Development programmes in 10 regions	
Digital skills in VET	Digital competence defined as a key competence	Further steps to be taken building on the adaptation of several modules to distance learning
	ICT module on basic digital competences development mandatory for all VET students, regardless of their specialisation	
	FabLabs established by GITA (see page 45) where VET students can develop digital skills, and FabLab ICT managers network created	Development of a Youth Coding and Tech Entrepreneurial club Networks (see below)
	Hackathons and "Boosters" organised by GITA	
	Increased availability of digital technologies in VET institutions (e.g. smartboards, simulators, occupational specific software)	
	International pilot self-assessment tool SELFIE in 15 VET schools	
	Some modules adapted to be delivered remotely after the COVID-19 crisis outbreak	
Promoting digital skills among the general population	Large awareness-raising activities led by the DGA, e.g. providing information and training on e-government services to public officials.	Implement programmes in education, innovation and e-government to encourage digital skills development and support the uptake of broadband services
	Digital literacy training targeted at citizens living in regions	
	Training on internet and e-commerce skills for disadvantaged citizens provided by the World Bank's GENIE programme (see Box 2.3)	
	Recognition since 2019 of non-formal learning outcomes, including for ICT related professions	Activities planned targeting disadvantaged groups (women, ethnic and social minorities, people with disabilities in targeted settlements)
	IT training centre for young people interested in ICT, offering regular training courses in programming, gaming, coding, graphic design	
	Development of digital literacy and citizen engagement centres in partner municipalities with GIZ support	

Source: OECD fact-finding questionnaires, June-August 2021 (OECD, 2021[96]), and desk research.

Fostering the uptake of digital technologies and services by SMEs

While favourable framework conditions are fundamental enablers of the digital economy, SMEs also need targeted support programmes to embrace their digital transformation. Indeed, SMEs' digital gap is due to their lack of awareness of the opportunities offered by new technologies, as well as their low levels of digital skills and limited resources to go digital (in terms of financial means, information and knowledge). This is a common feature across OECD and EaP countries, and is confirmed in the case of Georgia, where the local SME agency Enterprise Georgia quoted these issues as the main challenges for advancing the digital transformation of SMEs (OECD, 2021[96]).

In this regard, policymakers have a key role to play. SME agencies in particular are essential to provide such support programmes. In Georgia, GITA is responsible for implementing support measures for SME digitalisation. However, its actions focus on innovative start-ups and/or digital-by-default firms, and does not entail measures to help "traditional" SMEs adopt digital solutions. Other policy initiatives exist, but they appear scattered across different stakeholders (e.g. Enterprise Georgia that supports e-commerce practices, and the GCCI that launched e-commerce training). The following section takes stock of both financial and non-financial projects implemented so far.

Non-financial support

Georgian businesses benefit from an ecosystem built to encourage the digital transformation – but these infrastructure rather target firms that are developing an innovative digital product or service. In this respect, GITA acts as a business incubator, helping entrepreneurs scale up their disruptive ideas by offering them various products and services – from infrastructure (co-working spaces) to training, networking and financial support. As mentioned in Part 1, GITA has also developed 22 FabLabs across the country, three technology parks and five innovation centres (mini-tech parks). Three university-based innovation laboratories particularly foster skills development in programming and contribute to the organisation of events such as hackathons and Olympiads. Innovation infrastructure is to be further developed, notably through the GENIE project (Box 2.3), which has a component aiming at developing a network of regional innovation hubs and community innovation centres across the country.

Box 2.3 Georgia National Innovation Ecosystem (GENIE) project

Project overview

In March 2016, the Government of Georgia and the IBRD signed a five-year agreement, which has been extended by 23 months, i.e. until 2023, that granted Georgia 40 million USD to implement the GENIE project. This programme aimed at fostering the participation of individuals and firms in the digital economy and at increasing the number of innovative activities they perform. The project has been carried out by GITA.

The GENIE programme consists of four basic components, which frame and guide its action:

- Creation of innovation infrastructure to improve internet access, develop digital literacy and increase public awareness on broadband internet connection and its use;
- Ensure innovative support services, i.e. training and technical assistance to support digital skills development among individuals and firms;
- Funding of innovations through co-financing grant competitions directed at innovative companies and start-ups;
- Project implementation support

Selection of GENIE initiatives

Based on these components, GITA implemented a wide range of initiatives. A selection is presented below together with their results:

- Broadband-for-Development (BfD) programme to support the adoption and use of broadband by MSMEs and households, especially in rural areas;
- SMEs' e-commerce Capacity Building, which aims to deliver face-to-face training on digital skills, with a focus on e-commerce capacity development for BfD beneficiaries. However, a World Bank evaluation of the programme has highlighted its limited success for now: Internet is still predominantly used as an information source, and trainings hold a low participation rate – but more results could appear in the longer term. The evaluation's findings point to the need for a more comprehensive approach to ensure the effectiveness of the initiative;
- Regional Innovation Hubs (RIH) that allow access to co-working and prototyping facilities such as innovation labs;
- Community Innovation Centres (CICs), they allow innovative entrepreneurs from small cities and rural areas to access the appropriate infrastructure, services, and financing opportunities within the innovation ecosystem, by providing equipment, training and conferencing facilities, and co-working spaces;
- Innovation Matching Grant programme, i.e. financial support to projects that demonstrate innovation and market potential;
- Start-up Matching Grants Program, i.e. financial support to foster the creation of innovative enterprises;
- ICT training programme, that consists in a collaborative strategy to improve digital skills of Georgian professionals in one of the 30 fields covered (front-end programming, cybersecurity, project management, etc.), while preparing them for specific certifications. The goal is to train at least 3 000 participants by March 2023.

Source: (GITA, 2021[135]), (EU4Digital, 2020[136]), (GITA, 2018[137]), (World Bank Group, 2020[138]) and (World Bank, 2021[139]).

As a result, innovative, tech firms benefit from this constantly growing ecosystem, which also help them get an overview of the support services available. The above-mentioned technology parks for instance operate as one-stop-shops for IT companies and start-ups, promoting innovation and entrepreneurship while gathering technological, educational and professional resources in one physical space. Such a one-stop-shop does not exist for traditional firms looking to digitalise, which reduces the outreach of the services available, as SMEs are often not aware of existing solutions.

A growing number of initiatives support skills development, many of them aimed at equipping young people with advanced IT skills, to create a talent pool of IT specialists. This is the case of the above-mentioned ICT training programme within GENIE, and of the Youth Coding and Tech Entrepreneurial club networks, which are expected to form 2 000 students in programming and tech entrepreneurship and match them with mentors, IT and tech firms across eight target regions. Training on basic digital skills specifically for SMEs are also available on the Georgian market, although they remain rather scarce: GENIE's Broadband for Development Initiative for instance has trained about 1 500 SMEs in rural areas, notably on e-commerce, digital marketing and use of social networks and office programmes. Additional e-commerce training are offered by GITA within GENIE as well as by the GCCI: the latter designed the training programme based on the results of two needs assessments conducted among Georgian SMEs, and thereby trained over 600 business representatives on advertising products online, both on social media and online marketing platforms, between February and August 2021. The Chamber also provided individual aftercare services to businesses, and encouraged peer learning by inviting guest speakers from major e-commerce outlets and enterprises that successfully digitalised to share their experience. As mentioned in Part 1, it is supporting 100 businesses in developing their own website, and is developing, together with Georgian e-commerce experts, an e-book outlining guidelines for SME digitalisation, focusing on e-commerce practices. Building on this, these programmes could be scaled up and their impact better monitored. Indeed, such trainings are highly needed, notably to help firms improve their online sales: the Galt & Taggart report quotes the poor customer experience as a major challenge for Georgian e-commerce shops, resulting in local customers spending over three times more time on international online shops (Galt & Taggart, 2021[95]).

However, Georgia lacks advisory services. Entrepreneurs can receive free consultations on e-commerce development as part of the GENIE project, but none of the SME agencies nor private sector associations offer a comprehensive support programme to provide "traditional" firms substantial advice on how to go digital or similar resources. Moreover, only little is done to raise SMEs' awareness of the benefits of digitalisation. *Digitise Georgia* is one of the few awareness-raising initiatives implemented – it consists in training so-called "digital missionaries" in regions and develop their digital skills. These volunteers (about 300 so far) can then reach out to local businesses to help them ensure that they are covered on Google Maps with relevant information, including in English, thereby maximising their outreach among the population and tourists. However, there is no similar programme for other technologies – yet ensuring online presence through a dedicated website and/or social media platforms for instance is of crucial importance to increase customer outreach, and can improve the impact of Google Maps coverage.

Financial support

Financial support is another major pillar for SME digitalisation. Access to finance remains one of the main barriers for SMEs in general, for they encounter more difficulties to access financing than large firms – as outlined in Part 1. Their lack of resources partly explain their lower uptake of digital technologies, as these require both investments and relevant skills from managers and employees. Digital start-ups face similar financial issues because of the absence of local risk capital.

To tackle this funding issue, several programmes have been implemented by GITA to offer financial support to innovative SMEs, including digital ones. The co-financing grant programme for instance has financed 20 firms in 2021 for an overall amount of GEL 2 million. Throughout the years, financing initiatives have enabled the emergence of successful digital start-ups, such as Optio.AI, which was a beneficiary of the Matching Grant programme. The Georgian government continues to increase its expenditure on digital innovation, while working to attract foreign investments. As an example, an agreement was signed in 2020 between GITA, the NBG and *500 start-ups*, a leading US business accelerator, to launch the latter in Georgia and thereby contribute to the development of a regional ecosystem.

Initiatives to help traditional firms finance their digitalisation process are scarcer, mainly limited to Enterprise Georgia co-financing fees of placing products on digital marketplaces.

Way forward: Roadmap to accelerate SME digitalisation

Objective 1: Strengthen the institutional and policy framework for digitalisation

Adopt a comprehensive National Digital Strategy with clearly defined objectives, actions and resources

Almost all OECD countries have adopted a National Digital Strategy to ensure a comprehensive approach to the digital transformation (OECD, 2020[107]). Such strategies enable governments to define objectives and policy measures for the different aspects of digitalisation of economies and societies. By gathering them in one document, they allow for increased co-ordination between stakeholders. In that regard, Georgia should finalise and adopt its *Long-term National Strategy for the development of the digital economy and information society*, covering the various policy areas outlined below – from framework conditions to support programmes for SMEs, and related action plans containing clear measures, responsibilities, budget, timeframes and outcome indicators. The Strategy should be both robust, but allow enough flexibility to adapt to the fast-changing environment and changes in new technologies (OECD, 2017[140]).

Throughout the Strategy's development, it is of major importance to set up a co-ordination mechanism such as a dedicated working group including all public and private stakeholders (Ministries, relevant agencies, business associations), and ensure public-private consultations to take into account private sector's views. This will also contribute to an effective implementation of measures by stakeholders, while improving the co-ordination between them. Evaluations should also be carried out regularly to assess the policies' effectiveness, identify gaps and adjust accordingly.

Regarding emerging technologies, whose benefits for SMEs (see Table 2.1 and Box 2.1) remain largely untapped, a growing number of countries are establishing national AI strategies. Georgia could consider doing the same, as the country lags behind OECD levels in terms of policy framework for that technology. This shortcoming is reflected in the AI Government Readiness Index, where Georgia ranks 72 out of 172 countries analysed. As AI start-ups are emerging in the country, measures could be planned to establish a dedicated strategy that guides the adoption of this technology by providing legal, ethical and technical frameworks. Indeed, it is important to account for AI's far reaching and global implications that are likely to profoundly transform economies and societies (OECD, 2019[84]). Other emerging technologies such as IoT and Blockchain are not necessarily a policy priority, as they are still at a very nascent stage in Georgia as well as in other countries. Their benefits for firms are still being studied and remain so far less known than AI and, although these technologies offer a number of opportunities, they present a number of issues that have not been addressed yet and need to be accounted for. IoT can increase the likelihood of security incidents that can cause disruptions (OECD, 2018[85]), while Blockchain is characterized by high energy consumption, high costs and higher risks (Golosova and Romanovs, 2018[141]). Moreover, since many of the implications of these technologies have yet to be uncovered, the international community still lacks a common set of dedicated regulatory principles which is necessary for their effective use in cross-country operations such as supply chain. Nonetheless, policymakers should be aware of the latest developments in this regard, in order to be able to quickly respond to the constantly evolving conditions.

Task one of the existing SME support agencies with leading support for SME digitalisation

As noted above, Georgian firms do benefit from some support for digitalisation, but initiatives appear to be scattered across stakeholders. This is especially the case for the few services targeting "traditional" SMEs willing to go digital. These businesses would therefore need a "digital one-stop-shop", a single point of reference where they could seek information, advice and various resources on how to digitalise. Enterprise Georgia is well positioned to take this role, as the agency is already leading the overall support to SMEs and has developed extensive and valuable experience in helping firms from various sectors. Moreover, it has been working with the World Bank on developing measures to foster the digital transformation of SMEs within a recently launched five-year project, the *Georgia Relief and Recovery for MSMEs project*.

The chosen agency would need a strong mandate to lead initiatives on digitalisation. The latter could constitute a separate work stream for the chosen agency, with dedicated human and financial resources, and be easily identifiable in policy documents and external communication material such as governmental websites. The services to be offered by this one-stop-shop could include assessments of the state of digital maturity of different sectors, e.g. through surveys among firms of a given industry. This would enable stock taking of both the level of digital awareness and the uptake of digital technologies, in turn allowing for data collection on business practices by sector, as well as monitoring of the progress achieved. Moreover, the agency could list the financial and non-financial services available (see below) and ensure the co-ordination of resources and stakeholders. This would contribute to defining a clearer role for actors involved in the digital transformation, increase programmes' outreach, and ultimately increase efficiency of the related public policies.

Objective 2: Improve other framework conditions

Ensure broadband connectivity of higher quality and at lower prices

The NBDS foresees a wide range of measures to improve Internet access and notably to bridge the digital divides between urban and rural areas, which, despite improvements over the past years, remain an issue in Georgia. In order to further improve local broadband speed and affordability, especially of fixed broadband, and bring them closer to OECD levels, the government could consider the following:

- **Foster competition, investment and innovation**: in addition to adopting the draft *Law on Sharing Telecommunication Infrastructure and Physical Infrastructure Used for Telecommunication Purposes*, several measures could further support competition and, ultimately, faster Internet connection at lower prices. Georgia could improve multi-stakeholder dialogue on these issues through consultations between governmental bodies, network operators, regulatory authorities as well as consumers, in order to ensure that measures and regulations are understood, accepted and considering the views of all parties. This would help foster endorsement and avoid conflicts, such as the ones that followed the adoption of the *Law on Electronic Communications*. Moreover, periodical reviews of the legal and regulatory frameworks would help ensure its continued adequacy and detect if changes/improvements are needed (OECD, 2021[142]).
- **Strengthen the demand-side**: the NBDS has planned measures to support the demand-side through increased digital literacy. These provisions could be completed by measures to enhance consumer rights and choice, e.g. by eliminating information asymmetries. Ukraine offers an interesting example in this regard, having introduced several tools to build citizens' knowledge of broadband services and quality, such as an interactive map of telecommunication infrastructure and a free, online speed test for citizens to assess the quality of their Internet connection. In addition, collecting and making publicly available data on quality-of-service, including on network

outages, could not only inform users' choice, but also encourage network improvements. Ensuring effective dispute resolution mechanisms in case of conflict between a consumer and an Internet provider is another policy option.

Harmonise regulatory framework with EU standards to allow for more interoperability and exchanges with the EU market

Strengthening Georgia's legal and regulatory frameworks are of utmost importance to create conditions where individuals and businesses can make the most of the digital tools available while being protected from digital threats, breaches and personal data leaks. To this end, Georgia should:

- **Adopt a legal framework regulating e-commerce practices while enhancing consumer protection,** as required by the Association Agreement. The latter should align the national legislation with the EU e-commerce directive, the DCFTA requirements, and the new EU 2021 e-commerce package, e.g. on custom declaration and consumer protection, which is one of the main issues for cross-border transactions (EU4Digital, 2021[118]). The law should include provisions regarding e-payments, e.g. to ensure payment security and cap surcharges in transaction costs. The regulation would level the playing field, improving conditions for both consumers and businesses.

- **Align standards for e-signatures** with the EU eIDAS regulation while harmonising them with other EaP countries'.

Enhance digital security to build trust in the digital economy

Building on its existing policy framework, Georgia could further improve its citizens' trust in the digital economy by considering the following measures when preparing its third National Cybersecurity Strategy and related Action Plan:

- **Improve the policy framework for digital security**: Georgia could improve its detection and response capacity by empowering the existing CERT cert.gov.ge with more prerogatives, human and financial resources. The structure's website could be improve to serve as a platform to share information on digital risks, latest trends, and provide advice on preventive measures, thereby offering a centralised point of reference and contributing to raising awareness among individuals and firms. The same online platform could entail a feature for visitors to report incidents. Monitoring of digital security incidents could be improved to allow for more precise analyses and adapted responses, tailored to the most frequent types of attacks.

- **Foster the development of a digital security ecosystem**: co-operative measures appear to be one of Georgia's weakest indicators in the GCI 2020. Yet having a multi-stakeholder ecosystem for digital security is a key element to ensure an effective digital security management. Such co-operation can be fostered e.g. through sector-specific partnerships, and/or partnerships with Internet service providers to enhance the detection and response capacities (OECD, 2020[143]).

- **Step up awareness-raising initiatives** through dedicated training for firms, especially SMEs, to inform them of the different risks, help them minimise them by adopting good practices, teaching them how to respond, while improving their trust in online technologies. More generally, digital security should be taught to the general population as part of digital literacy trainings. Box 2.4 offers some good practice examples in this regard.

- **Complete the legal framework on digital security and data protection**: the current legislation could be updated to align with security requirements of the GDPR. The legal framework could incentivise firms to adopt a risk management approach. As for data protection, the amendments should notably introduce the once-only principle, frame data sharing and re-use, and introduce the obligation to notify data breaches.

Box 2.4. Toolbox for digital security policies

Facilitating reporting: Denmark's Common Digital Portal for Reporting

Within the Danish Cyber and information security strategy 2018-2021, the Danish authorities created a Common Digital Portal for Reporting, which allows businesses and authorities to report security incidents easily and quickly, and to receive contemporaneous information to act upon them and to prevent future threats. Several guidebooks are available in this regard. This reporting tool has been integrated to virk.dk, the country's one-stop-shop portal gathering all e-government services for businesses, making it easy for users to find and access.

Raising awareness: Cybersecurity Mexico

The Federal Government of Mexico has stepped up its awareness-raising initiatives since 2017 as part of its National Cybersecurity Strategy. The Federal Police notably implemented a National prevention campaign "Cybersecurity Mexico" to this end, which reached 680 000 citizens and generated more than 48 million interactions on social media. In addition to that, National Cybersecurity Weeks have been organised since 2015 in cooperation with the Organization of American States.

Education and training: Korea's Internet Security Agency (KISA)

KISA, launched in 2009, offers one of the most complete educational and professional training programmes to raise awareness among the population on Internet security. The agency provides trainings to foster the formation of security experts that can instantly respond to cyber-attacks, provide companies with the required protection depending on the industrial sector, and strengthen response capacities. These abilities are then certified through the Information Security National Technical Qualification Test. To establish an information security workforce, the programme supports undergraduate and graduate university courses that train future talents, and organises hacking defence competitions to discover the next-generation experts. KISA also provides seminars on cybersecurity for SMEs employees and school students. Moreover, as part of the Global project, KISA promotes international cooperation in the fight against cyber threats, offering invitation-based trainings for other countries on incidents response and the adoption of dedicated policies.

Source: (OECD, 2021[89]), (The Danish Government. Ministry of Finance, 2017[144]), (Council of Europe, 2020[145]) and (KISA. Korea Internet and Security Agency, 2021[146]).

Foster digital skills development

Georgia has already taken a certain number of steps to foster digital skills development at all levels of education and has planned additional measures in the NBDS, the Unified Strategy of Education and Science 2022-2032 and the VET Strategy 2021-2025. In addition to the recommendations and good practice examples provided in Part 1 of the present report, the government could consider the following actions to address the persisting digital skills shortcomings and skills mismatch in the labour market:

- **Regularly assess digital skills needs**: in order to tailor its trainings to market needs and ensure an increase of participants' employability, Georgia should conduct on a regular basis digital skills needs assessments. The SME agency, once designated as the digital one-stop-shop, could be responsible for this task. This could be done building on Enterprise Georgia's experience in the area of training needs analysis, as the agency conducted, with the support of the European Training Foundation, several quantitative and qualitative employer surveys over the past years.

- **Improve digital competences of teachers**, as these have been identified as one of the main shortcomings in the above-mentioned SELFIE assessment.

- **Raise awareness of the available training offer through a single-window portal**: the current initiatives to train citizens and firms in digital skills appear scattered across SME agencies, business associations and firms. Gathering them in a single place, e.g. on a governmental website, would help maximise their outreach. Such online platform could also enable participants to provide feedback on the quality of the trainings and skills acquired.

- **Foster the development of an ecosystem while ensuring a co-ordinated approach**: the many stakeholders acting upon digital literacy policies, such as industry players, intermediaries (clusters, business associations, etc.) and education providers, could be mapped and the links between them strengthened. This would allow for more co-ordination between initiatives, an increased public-private cooperation notably to design courses, and resource sharing within and across sectors.

- **Monitor and evaluate the impact of the policies and programmes implemented**: the recently adopted SME development strategy for instance plans to pursue GCCI's trainings on digital skills. Upon OECD advice, outcome indicators to assess the efficiency of these trainings have been included in the logical framework. Such evaluations should be carried out regularly and apply to all similar initiatives in order to ensure high-quality programmes. They could also help introduce certification mechanisms, as suggested in Part 1 (Box 1.2).

Objective 3: Develop comprehensive support for the digitalisation of non-IT sectors

Finally, Georgia needs to build a thorough understanding of SME digitalisation, beyond innovation and IT sector. The substantial support provided by GITA to innovative start-ups and digital firms, which has been bearing fruits and leading to the emergence of successful digital companies should be completed by comprehensive support measures for "traditional" firms, in order to enable the latter to reap the benefits of the digital transformation. To this end, the designated digital one-stop-shop should (i) raise SMEs' awareness of opportunities and digitalisation benefits, thereby tackling SMEs' lack of knowledge and information; (ii) accompany firms in carrying out an assessment of their digital maturity and identifying their needs; (iii) provide a range of non-financial solutions that can be tailored to the firm's needs, as diagnosed; (iv) introduce financial tools to support SMEs' uptake of digital technologies and (v) foster the effective development of an ecosystem for the digital transformation.

Figure 2.14 drafted based on OECD analysis of international best practices, provides a "blueprint" to design the policy instruments to respond to SME needs and facilitate their digital transformation.

Figure 2.14. A policymaker's blueprint to accelerate the digital transformation of SMEs

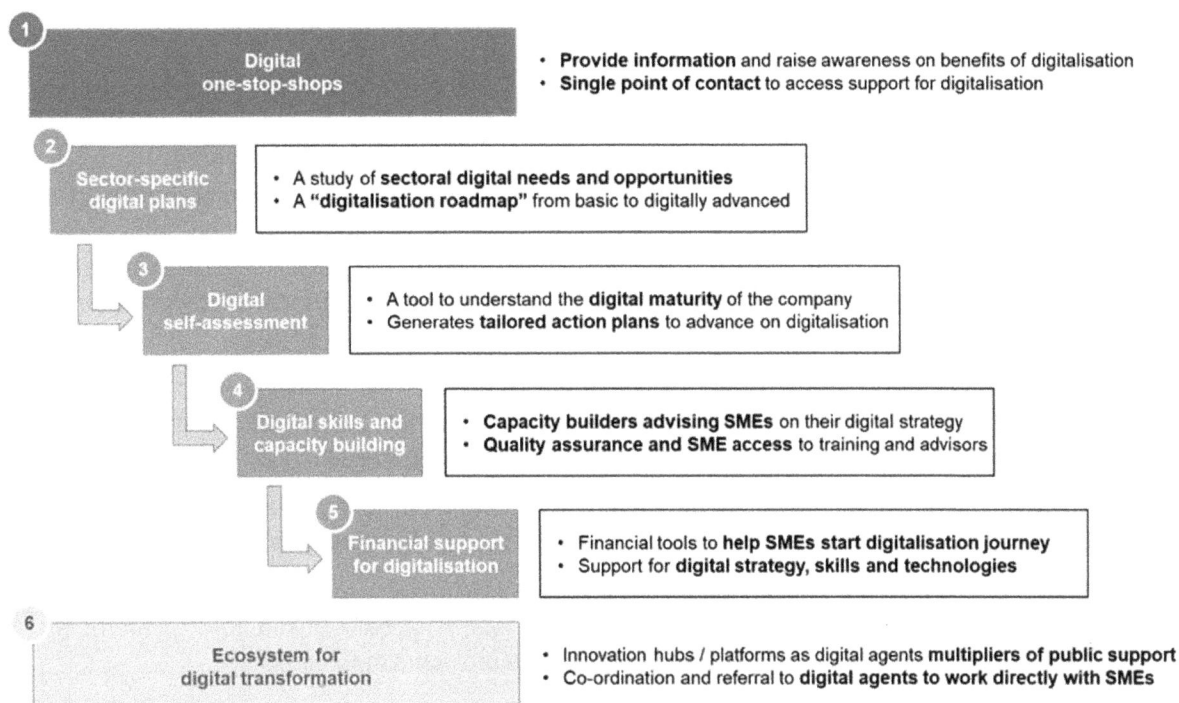

① Digital one-stop-shops
- **Provide information** and raise awareness on benefits of digitalisation
- **Single point of contact** to access support for digitalisation

② Sector-specific digital plans
- A study of **sectoral digital needs and opportunities**
- A **"digitalisation roadmap"** from basic to digitally advanced

③ Digital self-assessment
- A tool to understand the **digital maturity** of the company
- Generates **tailored action plans** to advance on digitalisation

④ Digital skills and capacity building
- **Capacity builders advising SMEs** on their digital strategy
- **Quality assurance and SME access** to training and advisors

⑤ Financial support for digitalisation
- Financial tools to **help SMEs start digitalisation journey**
- Support for **digital strategy, skills and technologies**

⑥ Ecosystem for digital transformation
- Innovation hubs / platforms as digital agents **multipliers of public support**
- Co-ordination and referral to **digital agents to work directly with SMEs**

Source: OECD analysis.

Raise awareness of the benefits of digitalisation and build a digital culture among SMEs

Raising awareness is the first step to SME digitalisation. As explained above, SMEs' lack of knowledge of the digital technologies available and of their benefits is one of the factors widening the gap between them and large firms. They often see digitalisation as a cost factor rather than an opportunity. The agency chosen as digital one-stop-shop should implement initiatives to overcome this issue. These could be expert webinars, workshops, dedicated events featuring successful examples of digital transformation in different sectors, and/or focused on one specific technology. Material solutions can also be useful, such as learning platforms and handbooks. Finland for instance has successfully implemented a wide range of such tools (Box 2.5).

Box 2.5. Raising awareness of the benefits of digitalisation among entrepreneurs: the case of the Federation of Finnish Enterprises (FFE)

The FFE is Finland's largest business association, including more than 115 000 Finnish enterprises within local and regional associations, and aiming at improving entrepreneurial conditions.

Finland is one of the most advanced countries in terms of SME digitalisation, as about 80% of the country's SMEs use basic digital tools on a daily basis. The gap between small and large firms is however significant when it comes to more advanced technologies and digitalisation of processes. The FFE has therefore implemented a number of support measures to raise awareness of the opportunities digital tools and technologies can bring, which include:

- *Entrepreneur's Digital School*, as mentioned in Box 1.2, i.e. the annual series of events that takes place in the main cities, bringing case examples and motivational peer learning activities, targeting small business owners that have just started the digitalisation process;

- Webinars, directed also to SMEs outside the organisation, to provide low-cost and easy-access training on the utilisation and application of the latest digital tools;

- *Entrepreneur's Digital Guidebook*, an online and free manual on different aspects of the business' digitalisation process. The guidebook is thematically linked to a platform that connects SMEs willing to digitise and digital service providers in Finland;

- *Entrepreneur's GDPR Handbook* that assists SMEs in meeting the requirements of the EU data protection regulation;

- *Entrepreneur's Media*, a print and digital media outlet that allows reaching a large number of small-business owners on a daily basis, to inform and inspire them on the latest digital developments and on the potential applications of digital tools.

Source: (SMeunited, 2019[147]), (OECD, 2021[148]) and (Suomen Yrittäjät, 2021[149]).

Enable firms to carry out a diagnosis of their digital maturity and needs assessment

Another way to raise SMEs' awareness while tailoring the support offered to their needs is to help them carry out a diagnosis of where they stand in the digitalisation process. Several tools can be introduced to this end:

- **A digital self-assessment tool**: many OECD countries, such as Austria, France and Luxembourg (quoted in Box 1.2), have introduced online questionnaires that companies can fill in within a short amount of time to estimate how digitally mature they are. Such test can include questions on the adoption of traditional technologies, such as CRM, SCM, social media, etc., but can also contain a sector-specific section focusing on the particular trends in a given industry. Upon completion of the test, the platform can generate a digitalisation percentage as well as initial recommendations on how to move forward. This tool not only enables entrepreneurs to assess themselves while learning about the technologies available for their sectors, but the results generated can also be used to collect anonymous data on SME digitalisation, allowing for more evidence-based policymaking.

- **Advisory services** under the form of an appointment with a specialised consultant: consultations with digitalisation experts can be introduced separately or as a complement to the self-assessment tool. In the second case, the entrepreneur can book an appointment with a specialised consultant: the latter can provide help in filling out the questionnaire, who can provide more explanation regarding the questions, and then discuss their results and the way forward, allowing for more explanation, exchanges, and better-tailored recommendations. The Austrian initiative KMU Digital offers an interesting example in this regard (see Box 2.6).

● **Sector-specific plans** can be developed and used as a reference to assess the level of digital maturity of a firm. The complexity of the digitalisation process does not allow for the emergence of a "one-size-fits-all" approach as businesses differ in products and services, goals and resources. However, some common features can be found within a given sector, e.g. tourism and catering. Recommender Systems for instance can be particularly relevant for tourism: this technology, based on data analytics, can direct customers towards the services that best fit their current needs and preferences, thereby reducing time, cost, and improving quality and satisfaction rates. Establishing sector-specific plans including step-by-step recommendations and a list of existing capabilities and trainings could constitute a useful source and point of reference for both for businesses and digitalisation consultants. As an example, Singapore created such plans within its *SME Go Digital Initiative*, which offers sector-specific Industry Digital Plans, i.e. step-by-step guides for SMEs containing digital solutions and training for employees tailored to the firm's needs, as well as recommendations.

Box 2.6. Supporting SMEs in their digitalisation journey: the case of KMU Digital

Programme overview

Launched in 2017 by the Austrian Federal Ministry for Digital and Economic Affairs and the Federal Austrian Economic Chamber, this public-private programme aims at supporting the digital transformation of SMEs in all its phases, offering

- An analysis of the firm's potential (4 hours, financed at 80%);
- Help in designing a digitalisation strategy (2 days, financed at 50%);
- Help in implementing the strategy (financed at 30%).

KMU Digital provides consulting services, from a free online self-assessment check and free analysis by consultants to advisory services and trainings for entrepreneurs and their employees. It also organises events and webinars on various topics, notably advanced technologies (e.g. blockchain, industrial IoT, etc.).

The role of certified consultants

One of the programme's success factors lies in the training and certification of local consultants, technology companies and agencies, resulting in an expert map publicly available (https://firmen.wko.at/suche_kmudigital).

On one side, the programme provides financial support to hire a certified consultant, covering a number of topics: business models and processes, e-commerce and online marketing, IT and cybersecurity, and digital administration. The consultation process is structured in two stages: first to guide the entrepreneurs in determining the company's opportunities, and then help them defining a strategic implementation plan. Following the sessions, consultants are required to document their work in a structured report that contains further recommendations for the entrepreneur. The reports delivered by consultants simultaneously provide valuable insights on digital trends in the country, including by firm size, sector, and region for instance.

On the other side, KMU tries to gather consultants that can provide their services, and to support them in strengthening their skills. Consultants are not only provided with webinars and trend cards to inform them of the programme and the latest technological developments, but they also receive information on available grants to further their professional development.

Outcome

Since its establishment, KMU Digital has supported around 15 000 digital transformation projects, and in March 2020, a survey of funding recipients confirmed an overall high level of satisfaction. Nearly 800 consultants have been trained and certified. The programme has been renewed in 2021, and it is now planned to continue until 2023.

Source: (WKO, 2021[150]), (SMeunited, 2019[147]), and exchanges with KMU Digital.

Provide SMEs with non-financial solutions tailored to their needs

Once a diagnosis has been made, SMEs need to have access to relevant resources and support to act upon the shortcomings identified and implement the action plan ensuing from the preliminary assessment.

Among the options for capacity building instruments, Georgia could consider:

- **Providing relevant trainings**: Georgia could scale up and expand its training initiatives in the field of digitalisation based on the needs identified by the self-assessments and sector-specific plans.

- **Developing a network of certified consultants and advisors**: in order to deliver quality advisory/consulting services and improve consumers' trust in them, the SME agency acting as the digital one-stop-shop could identify and train specialised consultants and advisors who could help SMEs in their digitalisation journey, from needs assessment to digitalisation strategy design and implementation. To this end, a mechanism should be implemented to certify the competences of these experts and thereby ensure that they meet certain quality standards – as done by the KMU Digital initiative described above (Box 2.6). In that regard, the existing infrastructure ecosystem of Fablabs, technology parks, etc., could play a role in building up and certifying expert knowledge with consultants or local communities. In addition, policymakers could facilitate SMEs' access to these services by co-financing or subsidising the costs of the services. Moldova's SME agency ODIMM for instance offers vouchers worth up to LEU 20 000 (EUR 975) for accessing such consulting services.

- **Mapping and promoting existing market solutions**: encouraged by GITA's many support measures implemented for them, a significant number of Georgian start-ups offering B2B solutions for the digital transformation, such as the previously mentioned B2C.ge and Optio.ai, has been emerging over the past five years. Table 2.3 provides a non-exhaustive list of examples. These market solutions help firms in their digital journey. It would therefore be beneficial to promote them, for instance through an online portal created and managed by the digital one-stop-shop and listing existing solutions – following the example of Start-up Friendly, GITA's platform linking start-ups and large businesses, or of the official website of the Business and Technology University btu.edu.ge, which has a section dedicated to start-ups. This measure would facilitate, at low cost, the connection between firms seeking to digitalise and start-ups offering relevant solutions, and thereby be mutually beneficial, as it would simultaneously foster the expansion of these digital start-ups, which often lack marketing and advertisement.

Table 2.3. Examples of existing market solutions for SME digitalisation in Georgia

Company name	Year created	Product	Examples of application sector	Supported by a governmental programme?	Website
Pulsar.AI	2016	Natural Language Processing (NLP) technologies for different languages. Acquired in 2021 by the US company SpinCar.	Mobile banking Automotive Retail Industry	Yes (GITA, through Start-up Matching Grant 2019)	Grant agreement between GITA and Pulsar AI
Touch	2016	Platform that unites international networks and local community to share how they work with newly developed digital tools	Support start-up development Companies' digitalisation	No	Touch Platform
Maxin AI	2017	IT consulting, offers a variety of solutions: chatbots, recommendation systems, conversion predictors, named entity recognition tools, user behaviour prediction tools, adult content filters, etc.	Digital solutions for companies issues	No	About Us - MaxinAI
Kernel	2020	A cloud-based financial management and planning software for early stage ventures	Companies' financial management – invoicing	Yes (GITA, through Start-up Matching Grant 2020)	https://kerneltools.com/ka/home-ka/#pll_switcher

Company name	Year created	Product	Examples of application sector	Supported by a governmental programme?	Website
Multi	2011	Counting, matching and analysis to help individuals and SMEs to manage their assets (inventories and Personal Protective Equipment) in live mode	Companies' resource management	Yes (GITA, through Start-up Matching Grant 2020)	Multi Solutions Group. (msgroup.ge)
Gymstinct	n/a	Fitness/wellness club management SaaS and plug & play facility access hardware (RFID Readers, turnstile controllers and locker system)	Fitness and wellness	Yes (GITA, through Start-up Matching Grant 2020)	(gymstinct.com)
Logmind	2018	AI-based log-data analytics platform, which will help DevOps and IT operational groups of large organisations to automatically detect errors in their applications	Solve IT errors within large companies	Yes (GITA, through Start-up Matching Grant 2019)	Logmind | AI-accelerated Log Data Analytics
Phubber	n/a	A mobile app that mixes social networking and online shopping for clothes. It already gathers more than 80 000 buyers and sellers.	Clothing market	Yes (GITA, through Start-up Matching Grant 2019)	https://beta.phubber.ge
Bizon	n/a	Platform where individuals and business entities are able to share (sell, rent, auction) machinery, equipment, and basic means among each other	Machinery and equipment market	Yes (GITA, through Start-up Matching Grant 2019)	(bizon.ge)

Increase financial support options for the digitalisation of "traditional" firms

Moreover, SMEs' access to finance should be facilitated, as this remains one of the main issues impeding their development. Various financial tools can be created to support the digitalisation of traditional firms. Most of them are similar to mechanisms that Georgia has already implemented in the past, but for other types of beneficiaries – e.g. grants such as GITA's Matching grant programme, where the applicant still co-finances part of the budget to ensure some private investment and share risks. Such scheme could be replicated for non-digital firms. Likewise, vouchers have been granted as part of the GENIE project to foster the uptake of broadband among businesses: similar instruments could be introduced to encourage SME managers' use of trainings and advisory services, as done by ODIMM in Moldova.

Ensure coordination and cooperation within the digitalisation ecosystem

Finally, the digital one-stop-shop should coordinate the different public and private stakeholders involved in SME digitalisation (Ministries, dedicated infrastructure such as incubators, accelerators, techparks, etc.). To this end, the agency should keep track of all initiatives aimed at accelerating the digital transformation, in order to ensure complementarity, avoid duplicates and optimise resources. In this context, the role of business associations should not be overlooked. They can provide expertise to guide SMEs in the digitalisation process, but also serve as coordinating agents among the multitude of stakeholders involved, create opportunities for networking, and inform policymakers of the needs and interests of their members. Some of the business associations active in Georgia have started offering some support to SME digitalisation: GCCI for example provides vocational courses to strengthen digital skills among its members; the Georgian Small and Medium Enterprises Association (GSMEA) invites expert members to inform interested SMEs on the latest legislative developments and share best practices, and Business Association of Georgia (BAG) organises networking opportunities for entrepreneurs of different sectors, an initiative that can promote knowledge exchange. Building on this, the involvement of these business associations should hence be encouraged, by giving visibility to their initiatives through the one-stop-shop, and by making use of their valuable experience in the design and implementation of new programmes.

The Malta Chamber of SMEs for example has actively supported the government in designing a grant scheme to help SMEs develop an e-commerce platform. In particular, since the application for the grant required a high volume of documents, including business plans, it has supported the adoption of an additional grant scheme that would provide SMEs with the necessary resources and expertise to comply with the requirements, making the programme more effective and easily accessible (SMeunited, 2019[147]).

References

Acelera PYMA (n.d.), *Acelera PYMA*, https://acelerapyme.gob.es/ (accessed on [37]
22 February 2021).

BCG (2020), *Ten Digital Moves for a Quick Performance Boost*, [81]
https://www.bcg.com/publications/2020/ten-digital-moves-for-quick-performance-boost
(accessed on 11 August 2021).

Blanchard, O., T. Philippon and J. Pisani-Ferry (2020), *20-8 A New Policy Toolkit Is Needed as* [42]
Countries Exit COVID-18 Lockdowns, Peterson Institute for International Economics,
https://www.piie.com/publications/policy-briefs/new-policy-toolkit-needed-countries-exit-covid-
19-lockdowns (accessed on 3 September 2020).

Communication Commission (2021), *Annual Report 2020*, [111]
https://comcom.ge/uploads/other/8/8000.pdf.

Council of Europe (2020), *Mexico: National cybersecurity strategy and awareness campaign*, [145]
https://www.coe.int/en/web/cyberviolence/-/mexico-national-cybersecurity-strategy-and-
awareness-campaign#91238255_91237754_True (accessed on 29 September 2021).

Council of the European Union (2020), *Council Conclusions on Regulatory sandboxes and* [45]
experimentation clauses as tools for an innovation-friendly, future-proof and resilient
regulatory framework that masters disruptive challenges in the digital age,
https://data.consilium.europa.eu/doc/document/ST-13026-2020-INIT/en/pdf.

Danube Transnational Programme (2021), *DanubeChance2.0*, http://www.interreg- [21]
danube.eu/approved-projects/danubechance2-0 (accessed on 1 June 2021).

Deloitte (2018), *Managing Risk in Digital Transformation*, [86]
https://www2.deloitte.com/content/dam/Deloitte/in/Documents/risk/in-ra-managing-risk-in-
digital-transformation-1-noexp.pdf.

Digital Luxembourg (n.d.), *DigiCheck: digital assessment tool | Digital Luxembourg*, [35]
https://digital-luxembourg.public.lu/initiatives/digicheck-digital-assessment-tool (accessed on
22 February 2021).

Early Warning Europe (2021), *Early Warning Denmark*, [20]
https://www.earlywarningeurope.eu/about/best-practices/early-warning-denmark (accessed
on 1 June 2021).

Economic Intelligence Unit (2019), *Country Report: Georgia 4th Quarter 2019*, [3]
http://www.eiu.com/FileHandler.ashx?issue_id=878841871&mode=pdf.

Enterprise Singapore (2021), *Go Global*, https://www.enterprisesg.gov.sg/keepgrowing/go-global (accessed on 4 November 2021). [53]

EU4Business (2021), *The Eastern Partnership Trade Helpdesk: Key Updates*, https://eu4business.eu/news/the-eastern-partnership-trade-helpdesk-key-updates/ (accessed on 14 September 2021). [52]

EU4Digital (2021), *E-commerce report: Recommendations proposed for eCommerce environment harmonisation in the EaP countries: Georgia*, https://eufordigital.eu/wp-content/uploads/2021/04/eCommerce-report-%E2%80%93-Recommendations-proposed-for-eCommerce-environment-harmonisation-in-the-EaP-countries-Georgia.pdf. [118]

EU4Digital (2021), *EU4Digital Telecom Rules Factsheet*, https://eufordigital.eu/wp-content/uploads/2020/09/EU4Digital-Telecom-Rules-Factsheet.pdf. [113]

EU4Digital (2021), *Harmonising digital markets in the Eastern Partnership*, https://europa.eu/capacity4dev/eu4digital/news/eu4digital-launches-ecommerce-pilot-automated-exchange-ecommerce-data-through-virtual-warehouse (accessed on 23 September 2021). [54]

EU4Digital (2020), *Building digital trust with the eSignature pilot initiative*, https://eufordigital.eu/building-digital-trust-with-the-esignature-pilot-initiative/ (accessed on 15 September 2021). [123]

EU4Digital (2020), *Cybersecurity guidelines for the Eastern Partner countries*, EU4Digital, https://www.euneighbours.eu/sites/default/files/publications/2020-12/Cybersecurity-guidelines-for-the-Eastern-Partner-countries.pdf. [131]

EU4Digital (2020), *Digital innovation SMEs' access to finance: policy recommendations: Georgia*, https://eufordigital.eu/wp-content/uploads/2020/07/Digital-innovation-SMEs%E2%80%99-access-to-finance-Policy-recommendations-Georgia.pdf. [43]

EU4Digital (2020), *Gap assessment of Georgia regulatory system in the field of electronic communications*, https://eufordigital.eu/wp-content/uploads/2021/04/Gap-assessment-of-Georgia-regulatory-system-in-the-field-of-electronic-communications.pdf. [114]

EU4Digital (2020), *Georgia: new innovation programme to train 3,000 in digital skills – apply before 30 November*, https://eufordigital.eu/georgia-new-innovation-programme-to-train-3000-in-digital-skills-apply-before-30-november/ (accessed on 22 September 2021). [136]

EU4Digital (2020), *How the pandemic accelerated the introduction of digital services in Georgia*, https://eufordigital.eu/how-the-pandemic-accelerated-the-introduction-of-digital-services-in-georgia/ (accessed on 7 September 21). [103]

EU4Digital (2020), *How women can change the field of innovation in Georgia*, https://eufordigital.eu/how-women-can-change-the-field-of-innovation-in-georgia/ (accessed on 28 February 2021). [72]

EU4Digital (2019), "Georgia introduces mandatory electronic signatures for online public transactions", *EU4Digital*, https://eufordigital.eu/georgia-introduces-mandatory-electronic-signatures-for-online-public-transactions/ (accessed on 14 September 2021). [121]

European Commission (2020), *Fight against COVID-19 | European Vocational Skills Week*, https://ec.europa.eu/social/vocational-skills-week/fight-against-covid-19_en (accessed on 22 February 2021). [34]

European Commission (2017), *Better Regulation Toolbox*, https://ec.europa.eu/info/sites/default/files/better-regulation-toolbox_1.pdf. [22]

European Construction Sector Observatory (2021), *Digitalisation in the Construction Sector*, https://www.google.com/url?sa=t&rct=j&q=&esrc=s&source=web&cd=&ved=2ahUKEwi5oLX8mv_zAhUE1xoKHbQWDXoQFnoECAUQAQ&url=https%3A%2F%2Fec.europa.eu%2Fdocsroom%2Fdocuments%2F45547%2Fattachments%2F1%2Ftranslations%2Fen%2Frenditions%2Fpdf&usg=AOvVaw1k1qK2ZjTCSkJk1. [92]

European Training Foundation (2021), *New Forms of Employment in the Eastern Partnership Countries: Platform Work - Georgia*, https://www.etf.europa.eu/sites/default/files/2021-06/platform_work_georgia_0.pdf. [32]

FabLab Georgia (2021), *FabLab Georgia*, http://fablab.gov.ge/eng/static/43/saqartvelos-fablabebi (accessed on 20 October 2021). [25]

Gal, P. et al. (2019), "Digitalisation and productivity: In search of the holy grail – Firm-level empirical evidence from EU countries", Vol. 1533, https://doi.org/https://doi.org/10.1787/5080f4b6-en. [152]

Galt & Taggart (2021), *E-commerce in Georgia*, https://galtandtaggart.com/en/reports/research-reports/e-commerce-georgia. [95]

GeoLab (2021), *WHAT IS GeoLab?*, http://www.geolab.edu.ge/en-US/Home/Environment. [60]

Georgian National Blockchain Agency (2018), *Partners*, https://gnba.ge/en/#psc-partners (accessed on 15 September 2021). [100]

Geostat (2021), *Export - National Statistics Office of Georgia*, https://www.geostat.ge/en/modules/categories/637/export (accessed on 24 July 2021). [47]

Geostat (2021), *Information and Communication Technologies Usage in Households*, https://www.geostat.ge/en/modules/categories/106/information-and-communication-technologies-usage-in-households. [116]

German Economic Team (2021), *Return to growth path after crisis year*, https://www.german-economic-team.com/georgien/wp-content/uploads/sites/3/GET_GEO_NL_41_2021_en.pdf. [7]

German Economic Team (2019), *Economic Monitor Georgia*, https://www.german-economic-team.com/georgien/wp-content/uploads/sites/3/GET_GEO_EM_10_2019_en.pdf. [2]

GIPA (2021), *Innovation Laboratory's presentation CG MULTILAB*, https://gipa.ge/eng/list/show/422-Innovation-Laboratorys-presentation-CG-MULTILAB (accessed on 21 October 21). [62]

GITA (2021), *GENIE*, https://gita.gov.ge/eng/static/31/genie (accessed on 22 September 2021). [135]

GITA (2021), *ILabs*, https://gita.gov.ge/eng/static/51/ilab-ebi (accessed on 21 October 2021). [59]

GITA (2021), *IT Trainings*, https://gita.gov.ge/eng/static/125/it (accessed on 20 October 2021). [132]

GITA (2021), *Techparks and innovation centers*, https://gita.gov.ge/eng/static/45/teknoparki-tbilisi (accessed on 29 July 2021). [58]

GITA (2018), *Georgian MSMEs' E-commerce Capacity Building*, https://gita.gov.ge/geo/list/show/81-Georgian-MSMEs-E-commerce-Capacity-Building (accessed on 22 September 2021). [137]

GIZ (2020), *SME DEVELOPMENT AND DCFTA IN GEORGIA. Enabling Georgian entrepreneurs to benefit from the free trade agreement with the EU. Project achievements 2015-2019*, Deutsche Gesellschaft für Internationale Zusammenarbeit (GIZ) GmbH, https://www.euneighbours.eu/sites/default/files/publications/2020-04/smedcftage_finalreport_dp_0.pdf. [50]

Going Digital Toolkit Policy Note, N. (ed.) (2020), *The role of sandboxes in promoting flexibility and innovation in the digital age*, https://goingdigital.oecd.org/toolkitnotes/the-role-of-sandboxes-in-promoting-flexibility-and-innovation-in-the-digital-age.pdf. [44]

Golosova, J. and A. Romanovs (2018), "The Advantages and Disadvantages of the Blockchain Technology", *2018 IEEE 6th Workshop on Advances in Information, Electronic and Electrical Engineering (AIEEE)*, http://dx.doi.org/10.1109/AIEEE.2018.8592253. [141]

Google LLC (2021), *Google COVID-19 Community Mobility Reports*, https://www.google.com/covid19/mobility/ (accessed on 1 September 2021). [94]

Government of Georgia (2021), *Draft SME Development Strategy of Georgia 2021-2025*. [23]

Government of Georgia (2021), საქართველოს კიბერუსაფრთხოების 2021 – 2024 წლების ეროვნული სტრატეგიისა და მისი სამოქმედო გეგმის დამტკიცების შესახებ *[Approval of the National Cyber Security Strategy of Georgia 2021 - 2024 and its Action Plan]*, https://matsne.gov.ge/document/view/5263611?publication=0. [128]

Government of Georgia (2020), *Law of Georgia on Investment Funds*, https://matsne.gov.ge/en/document/view/4924135?publication=0 (accessed on 14 September 2020). [41]

Government of Georgia (2020), *Law of Georgia On Rehabilitation and the Collective Satisfaction of Creditors' claims*, https://matsne.gov.ge/ka/document/download/4993950/0/en/pdf. [18]

Government of Georgia (2020), *Measures Implemented by the Government of Georgia against COVID-19 Report*, https://stopcov.ge/Content/files/COVID_RESPONSE_REPORT__ENG.pdf. [102]

Government of Georgia (2020), *On the Approval of Regulatory Impact Assessment (RIA) Methodology*, https://www.matsne.gov.ge/en/document/view/4776100?publication=0 (accessed on 1 June 2021). [19]

Government of Georgia (2017), *Law On Electronic Documents and Electronic Trust Services*, https://matsne.gov.ge/en/document/view/3654557?publication=0 (accessed on 14 September 2021). [120]

Government of Georgia (2016), *Law on Innovations*, https://matsne.gov.ge/en/document/view/3322328?publication=0 (accessed on 25 February 2021). [57]

Government of Georgia (2012), *Cyber Security Strategy of Georgia 2012-2015*, https://sherloc.unodc.org/cld/uploads/res/lessons-learned/geo/cyber-security-strategy-of-georgia-2012-2015_html/National_Cyber_Security_Strategy_of_Georgia_ENG.pdf.

[126]

Government of Georgia (2008), *Law of Georgia on Electronic Signatures and Electronic Documents*, https://www.google.com/url?sa=t&rct=j&q=&esrc=s&source=web&cd=&cad=rja&uact=8&ved=2ahUKEwiO-d25nv7yAhWBzYUKHYEqCf0QFnoECAQQAQ&url=https%3A%2F%2Fmatsne.gov.ge%2Fru%2Fdocument%2Fdownload%2F20866%2F4%2Fen%2Fpdf&usg=AOvVaw3YKNwg0WoV4ALnCQ892cn4 (accessed on 14 September 2021).

[119]

Green Economy Financing Facility (2019), *EBRD and Partners Deepen Green Finance in Georgia*, https://ebrdgeff.com/ebrd-and-partners-deepen-green-finance-in-georgia/ (accessed on 20 October 2021).

[78]

Griessbach, L. and K. Ettl (2020), "The entrepreneurial ecosystem and its impact on female managers in transition economies: The case of Georgia", *Journal of East European Management Studies* Special issue, pp. 150-171.

[71]

Halabisky, D. (2018), *Policy Brief on Women's Entrepreneurship*, OECD Publishing, https://www.oecd-ilibrary.org/docserver/dd2d79e7-en.pdf?expires=1628285428&id=id&accname=ocid84004878&checksum=344C662D07DA050620B7CBB0233DD05B.

[75]

Heritage Foundation (2021), *Georgia Economy: Population, GDP, Inflation, Business, Trade, FDI, Corruption*, https://www.heritage.org/index/country/georgia.

[4]

Human Rights Education and Monitoring Center (2020), *Labor Market Segmentation and Informal Labour During Crisis*, https://www.google.com/url?sa=t&rct=j&q=&esrc=s&source=web&cd=&cad=rja&uact=8&ved=2ahUKEwiu2sz3iP_zAhVPUxoKHUyrAJQQFnoECAUQAQ&url=https%3A%2F%2Fwww.ge.undp.org%2Fcontent%2Fgeorgia%2Fen%2Fhome%2Flibrary%2Fdemocratic_governance%2Fcovid-labor-market-segmenta.

[31]

ILIA State University (2021), *GITA*, https://iliauni.edu.ge/en/iliauni/units/developmentoffice/mimdinare-proeqtebi/gita5 (accessed on 21 October 2021).

[61]

IMF (2021), *GEORGIA 2021 ARTICLE IV CONSULTATION—PRESS RELEASE; STAFF REPORT; AND STATEMENT BY THE EXECUTIVE DIRECTOR FOR GEORGIA*, https://www.imf.org/external/pubs/cat/longres.aspx?sk=465906.0.

[13]

IMF (2021), *Georgia: 2021 Article IV Consultation-Press Release; Staff Report; and Statement by the Executive Director for Georgia*, https://www.imf.org/-/media/Files/Publications/CR/2021/English/1GEOEA2021002.ashx (accessed on 5 October 2021).

[5]

IMF (2021), *Georgia: Staff Concluding Statement of the 2021 Article IV Mission*, https://www.imf.org/en/News/Articles/2021/07/16/mcs071921-georgia-staff-concluding-statement-of-the-2021-article-iv-mission (accessed on 5 October 2021).

[9]

IMF (2021), *World Economic Outlook Database*, https://www.imf.org/en/Publications/WEO/weo-database/2021/April (accessed on 30 September 2021). [12]

IMF (2021), *World Economic Outlook. Recovery During a Pandemic. Health Concerns, Supply Disruptions, and Price Pressures.*, https://www.imf.org/-/media/Files/Publications/WEO/2021/October/English/text.ashx. [14]

Infocomm Media Development Authority (2021), *Construction and Facilities Management*, https://www.imda.gov.sg/-/media/Imda/Files/Programme/SMEs-Go-Digital/Industry-Digital-Plans/Construction-and-Facilities-Management-IDP/Construction-and-Facilities-Management-IDP_v3.pdf. [93]

Infocomm Media Development Authority (2021), *Industry Digital Plans*, https://www.imda.gov.sg/programme-listing/smes-go-digital/industry-digital-plans (accessed on 22 February 2021). [36]

Innovation Finance Advisory (2020), *Funding Women Enterpreneurs. How to Empower growth*, https://www.eib.org/attachments/thematic/why_are_women_entrepreneurs_missing_out_on_funding_en.pdf. [74]

INSEAD (2020), *Global Innovation Index 2020 - Georgia*, https://www.wipo.int/edocs/pubdocs/en/wipo_pub_gii_2020/ge.pdf. [68]

INSEAD (2020), *The Global Innovation Index [database]*, https://www.globalinnovationindex.org/analysis-indicator (accessed on 3 August 2021). [64]

Institute for Development of Freedom and Information (2019), *Evaluation of the Extent and Quality of Public Private Dialogue in Georgia: 2014–2019*, IDFI, https://idfi.ge/en/quality_of_ppd_in_georgia. [16]

Intel (2021), *Top Use Cases for 5G Technology*, https://www.intel.com/content/www/us/en/wireless-network/5g-use-cases-applications.html (accessed on 4 November 2021). [91]

ITU (2021), *Global Cybersecurity Index 2020*, https://www.itu.int/dms_pub/itu-d/opb/str/D-STR-GCI.01-2021-PDF-E.pdf. [125]

ITU (2021), *ITU World Telecommunication/ICT Indicators Database 2021*, https://www.itu.int/en/ITU-D/Statistics/Pages/publications/wtid.aspx (accessed on 21 October 2021). [97]

ITU (2021), *Statistics*, https://www.itu.int/en/ITU-D/Statistics/Pages/stat/default.aspx (accessed on 4 May 2021). [108]

ITU (2020), *5G Country Profile - Georgia*, https://www.itu.int/en/ITU-D/Regional-Presence/Europe/Documents/Events/2020/5G_EUR_CIS/5G_Georgia-final.pdf. [110]

JobOutlook (2021), *Skills Match | JobOutlook*, https://joboutlook.gov.au/career-tools/skills-match#/ (accessed on 22 February 2021). [33]

KISA. Korea Internet and Security Agency (2021), *Main Activitries*, https://www.kisa.or.kr/eng/mainactivities/internetPromotion.jsp (accessed on 29 September 2021). [146]

Krabina, B. et al. (2017), *Digital Georgia (E-Georgia Strategy and Action Plan 2014-2018)*, https://fr.scribd.com/document/345908416/Digital-Georgia-e-Georgia-strategy-and-action-plan-2014-2018. [134]

Labour Market Information System (2020), *Survey of Business Demand on Skills 2020*, Ministry of Economy and Sustainable Development of Georgia, http://www.lmis.gov.ge/Lmis/Lmis.Portal.Web/Handlers/GetFile.ashx?Type=Content&ID=cfaa802f-c54e-4607-9875-69abaa284777 (accessed on 22 February 2021). [26]

Lomsadze, G. (2021), *COVID deepens digital divide in Georgian schools*, https://eurasianet.org/covid-deepens-digital-divide-in-georgian-schools (accessed on 7 September 2021). [104]

Ministry of Economic Development of Italy (2021), *Incentives to investors: Italy's Industria 4.0 plan*, https://investorvisa.mise.gov.it/index.php/en/home-en/incentives-to-investors-italy-s-industria-4-0-plan (accessed on 3 August 2021). [65]

Ministry of Education and Science of Georgia (2017), *Unified Strategy of Education and Science 2017-2021*, https://mes.gov.ge/content.php?id=7755&lang=eng (accessed on 22 February 2021). [24]

National Bank of Georgia (2019), *Annual report*, https://www.nbg.gov.ge/uploads/publications/annualreport/2020/annual_report_eng.pdf. [40]

National Bank of Georgia (2017), *Law on Payment Services*, https://nbg.gov.ge/en/page/law-on-payment-services (accessed on 13 September 2021). [101]

OECD (2021), *COVID-19 and greening the economies of Eastern Europe, the Caucasus and Central Asia*, https://www.oecd.org/coronavirus/policy-responses/covid-19-and-greening-the-economies-of-eastern-europe-the-caucasus-and-central-asia-40f4d34f/#figure-d1e182. [76]

OECD (2021), *Designing active labour market policies for the recovery*, https://www.oecd.org/coronavirus/policy-responses/designing-active-labour-market-policies-for-the-recovery-79c833cf/#section-d1e366. [30]

OECD (2021), *Main Science and Technology Indicators*, https://www.oecd.org/sti/msti.htm. [63]

OECD (2021), *Recommendation on Broadband Connectivity*, https://legalinstruments.oecd.org/en/instruments/OECD-LEGAL-0322 (accessed on 30 July 2021). [142]

OECD (2021), *Responses to fact-finding questions by EaP policymakers, June-September 2021 (unpublished)*. [96]

OECD (2021), *SME Enterpreneurship Policy in the Slovak Republic*, https://doi.org/10.1787/9097a251-en. [148]

OECD (2021), *The Digital Transformation of SMEs*, OECD Publishing, Paris, https://dx.doi.org/10.1787/bdb9256a-en. [89]

OECD (2020), *COVID-19 and international trade: Issues and actions*, OECD Publishing, https://www.oecd.org/coronavirus/policy-responses/covid-19-and-international-trade-issues-and-actions-494da2fa/. [51]

OECD (2020), *COVID-19 crisis response in Eastern Partner countries*, [6]
https://www.oecd.org/coronavirus/policy-responses/covid-19-crisis-response-in-eu-eastern-partner-countries-7759afa3/#section-d1e1210.

OECD (2020), *Keep the Internet up and running in times of crisis*, [106]
https://www.oecd.org/coronavirus/policy-responses/keeping-the-internet-up-and-running-in-times-of-crisis-4017c4c9/.

OECD (2020), *OECD Digital Economy Outlook 2020*, OECD Publishing, Paris, [107]
https://dx.doi.org/10.1787/bb167041-en.

OECD (2020), *OECD/INFE survey instrument to measure the financial literacy of MSMEs*, [46]
https://www.oecd.org/financial/education/2020-survey-to-measure-msme-financial-literacy.pdf.

OECD (2020), *Seven lessons learned about digital security during the COVID-19 crisis*, OECD [143]
Publishing, https://www.oecd.org/coronavirus/policy-responses/seven-lessons-learned-about-digital-security-during-the-covid-19-crisis-e55a6b9a/.

OECD (2020), *The potential of online learning for adults: Early lessons from the COVID-19 crisis*, [29]
https://www.oecd.org/coronavirus/policy-responses/the-potential-of-online-learning-for-adults-early-lessons-from-the-covid-19-crisis-ee040002/.

OECD (2020), *Trade Finance in Times of Crisis - Responses from Export Credit Agencies*, [55]
OECD Publishing, https://www.oecd.org/coronavirus/policy-responses/trade-finance-in-times-of-crisis-responses-from-export-credit-agencies-946a21db/#boxsection-d1e87.

OECD (2019), *FDI Restrictiveness Index*, OECD Publishing, [112]
https://stats.oecd.org/Index.aspx?datasetcode=FDIINDEX&_ga=2.133605134.1442833365.1621436300-161112846.1612458886#.

OECD (2019), *Going Digital: Shaping Policies, Improving Lives*, OECD Publishing, Paris, [80]
https://dx.doi.org/10.1787/9789264312012-en.

OECD (2019), *Recommendation of the Council on Artificial Intelligence*, [84]
https://legalinstruments.oecd.org/en/instruments/OECD-LEGAL-0449.

OECD (2019), *Trade facilitation indicators (database)*, https://www.oecd.org/trade/topics/trade-facilitation/ (accessed on 25 February 2021). [48]

OECD (2018), *Environmental Policy Toolkit for SME Greening in EU Eastern Partnership*, [79]
https://www.oecd-ilibrary.org/environment/environmental-policy-toolkit-for-sme-greening-in-eu-eastern-partnership-countries/environmental-regulatory-tools-in-oecd-and-eap-countries_9789264293199-6-en;jsessionid=dxKLVKzQgBNnmv6X2AJLLYs5.ip-10-240-5-71.

OECD (2018), "IoT measurement and applications", *OECD Digital Economy Papers*, No. 271, [85]
OECD Publishing, Paris, https://dx.doi.org/10.1787/35209dbf-en.

OECD (2018), *Mobilising Finance for Climate Action in Georgia*, https://www.oecd-ilibrary.org/finance-and-investment/mobilising-finance-for-climate-action-in-georgia_9789264289727-en. [77]

OECD (2018), *OECD Blockcahin Primer*, https://www.oecd.org/finance/OECD-Blockchain-Primer.pdf. [90]

OECD (2017), *Key recommendations for the G20*, https://www.oecd.org/g20/policy-recommendations-for-digital-transformation-in-the-G20.pdf. [140]

OECD (2017), *Public Procurement for Innovation: Good practices and strategies*, OECD Publishing, https://www.oecd-ilibrary.org/docserver/9789264265820-en.pdf?expires=1635847298&id=id&accname=ocid84004878&checksum=4683372152B103F277054E39DFAE6436 (accessed on 2 November 2021). [67]

OECD (2016), "Managing Digital Security and Privacy Risk", *OECD Digital Economy Papers*, No. 254, OECD Publishing, Paris, https://dx.doi.org/10.1787/5jlwt49ccklt-en. [124]

OECD (2016), *Preventing corruption in public procurement*, OECD Publishing, https://www.oecd.org/gov/ethics/Corruption-Public-Procurement-Brochure.pdf. [66]

OECD (2015), *Digital Security Risk Management for Economic and Social Prosperity: OECD Recommendation and Companion Document*, OECD Publishing, Paris, https://dx.doi.org/10.1787/9789264245471-en. [130]

OECD (2015), *Does having digital skills really pay off?*, https://doi.org/10.1787/5js023r0wj9v-en. [133]

OECD (2014), *Measuring the Digital Economy: A New Perspective*, OECD Publishing, Paris, https://dx.doi.org/10.1787/9789264221796-en. [88]

OECD (2011), *OECD Guide to Measuring the Information Society 2011*, OECD Publishing, Paris, https://dx.doi.org/10.1787/9789264113541-en. [87]

OECD et al. (2020), *SME Policy Index: Eastern Partner Countries 2020: Assessing the Implementation of the Small Business Act for Europe*, SME Policy Index, OECD Publishing, Paris/European Union, Brussels, https://dx.doi.org/10.1787/8b45614b-en. [1]

Optio.AI (2021), *Optio's Natural Language Processing Engine will power Bank of Georgia's virtual assistant*, https://www.optio.ai/index.php/2021/02/02/optios-natural-language-processing-engine-will-power-bank-of-georgias-virtual-assistant/ (accessed on 15 September 2021). [98]

Parliament of Georgia (2021), *Law of Georgia on Information Security*, https://matsne.gov.ge/en/document/view/1679424?publication=3. [129]

Parliament of Georgia (2020), *Legislative Herald of Georgia*, https://matsne.gov.ge/en/document/view/4892732?publication=0 (accessed on 14 September 2021). [122]

Santiso, C. (2021), "Digitalisation as an anti-corruption strategy: what are the integrity dividends of going digital?", *OECD Development Matters*, https://oecd-development-matters.org/2021/08/04/digitalisation-as-an-anti-corruption-strategy-what-are-the-integrity-dividends-of-going-digital/ (accessed on 28 October 2021). [82]

Small and Medium Telecom Operators Association of Georgia and Tusheti Development Fund (2018), *Say "No" to Isolation: The Tusheti Wi-Fi Community network in Georgia*, https://giswatch.org/en/country-report/infrastructure/georgia. [109]

Small Business Standards (2018), *E-Competence Framework: the SME way through the European standard on digital competencies*, https://www.digitalsme.eu/digital/uploads/SBS_brochure_v4.pdf. [38]

SMeunited (2019), *Best Practices on Assisting SMEs in the Digital Transformation*, https://www.smeunited.eu/admin/storage/smeunited/smeunited-digital-brochure.pdf. [147]

Sorbe, S. et al. (2019), "Digital Dividend: Policies to Harness the Productivity Potential of Digital Technologies", *OECD Economic Policy Papers*, No. 26, OECD. [105]

Statista (2021), *Digital Market Outlook*, Statista, https://www.statista.com/outlook/digital-markets. [117]

Suomen Yrittäjät (2021), *About Suomen Yrittäjät*, https://www.yrittajat.fi/en/about-suomen-yrittajat-526258 (accessed on 29 September 2021). [149]

The Danish Government. Ministry of Finance (2017), *Danish Cyber and Information Security Strategy, May 2018*, https://en.digst.dk/media/17189/danish_cyber_and_information_security_strategy_pdf.pdf. [144]

The World Bank (2021), *Restructuring Paper on a Proposed Project Restructuring ofe Georgia National Ecosystem (GENIE) Project approved on March 18, 2016*, https://documents1.worldbank.org/curated/en/244281605757611990/text/Disclosable-Restructuring-Paper-Georgia-National-Innovation-Ecosystem-GENIE-Project-P152441.txt. [151]

UN Women (2020), *Rapid Gender Assessment of the COVID-19 situation in Georgia*, UN Women, https://www2.unwomen.org/-/media/field%20office%20georgia/attachments/publications/2020/rga-unw.pdf?la=en&vs=143. [73]

UNDP (2021), *Digital solutions transform Georgia's public sector*, https://www.ge.undp.org/content/georgia/en/home/stories/electronic-services.html. [17]

UNDP (2020), *COVID-19 Global Gender Response Tracker - Factsheet: Europe and Central Asia, December 2020*, https://www.eurasia.undp.org/content/rbec/en/home/library/gender-equality/COVID19-Global-Gender-Response-Tracker.html. [70]

UNECE (2018), *Regulatory and Procedural Barriers to Trade in Georgia. Needs Assessment*, https://unece.org/fileadmin/DAM/trade/Publications/ECE_TRADE_443E_Georgia.pdf. [49]

United Nations (2019), *Report of Georgia on Resolution 73/27 on Developments in the field of information and telecommunications in the context of international security & 73/266 on Advancing responsible State behavior in cyberspace in the context of international security*, https://www.un.org/disarmament/wp-content/uploads/2019/08/georgia-73-27-73-266-dea-mod.pdf. [127]

USAID Georgia (2019), *Georgia's Innovation Strategy & Recommendations*, https://pdf.usaid.gov/pdf_docs/PA00TNC5.pdf. [56]

WKO (2021), *KMU.Digital*, https://www.kmudigital.at/Content.Node/kampagnen/kmudigital/the-austrian-digitalization-initiative-for-smes.html (accessed on 29 September 2021). [150]

World Bank (2021), *Development Indicators*, https://databank.worldbank.org/source/world-development-indicators (accessed on 30 September 2021). [11]

World Bank (2021), *Global Economic Prospects*, https://openknowledge.worldbank.org/bitstream/handle/10986/35647/9781464816659.pdf. [10]

World Bank (2021), *Restructuring Paper on a Proposed Project Restructuring ofe Georgia National Ecosystem (GENIE) Project approved on March 18, 2016*, https://documents1.worldbank.org/curated/en/244281605757611990/text/Disclosable-Restructuring-Paper-Georgia-National-Innovation-Ecosystem-GENIE-Project-P152441.txt. [139]

World Bank (2021), *The World Bank in Georgia*, https://www.worldbank.org/en/country/georgia/overview#3 (accessed on 3 November 2021). [8]

World Bank (2020), *Enterprise Surveys Follow-Up on COVID-19. Georgia 2020 - Round 2*, https://www.enterprisesurveys.org/en/covid-19 (accessed on 1 June 2021). [15]

World Bank (2019), *Enterprise Surveys Indicators Data - World Bank Group [database]*, https://www.enterprisesurveys.org/en/enterprisesurveys (accessed on 22 February 2021). [28]

World Bank Group (2020), *Promoting E-commerce in Georgia. Exploring Constraints to Online Participation using Baseline Data from an Experimental Study*, https://openknowledge.worldbank.org/bitstream/handle/10986/34226/Promoting-E-commerce-in-Georgia-Exploring-Constraints-to-Online-Participation-using-Baseline-Data-from-an-Experimental-Study.pdf?sequence=4&isAllowed=y (accessed on 20 October 2021). [138]

World Bank Group (2018), *Cryptocurenncies and Blockchain*, https://openknowledge.worldbank.org/bitstream/handle/10986/29763/9781464812996.pdf. [99]

World Economic Forum (2021), *Global Gender Gap Report 2021*, http://www3.weforum.org/docs/WEF_GGGR_2021.pdf. [69]

World Economic Forum (2020), *Hacking Corruption in the Digital Era: How Tech is Shaping the Future of Integrity in times of Crisis*, https://www3.weforum.org/docs/WEF_GFC_on_Transparency_and_AC_Agenda_for_Business_Integrity_pillar_3_2020.pdf. [83]

World Economic Forum (2020), *Network Readiness Index*, https://networkreadinessindex.org/countries/georgia/. [115]

World Economic Forum (2019), *The Global Competitiveness Report 2019*, World Economic Forum, http://reports.weforum.org/global-competitiveness-report-2019/. [27]

Yrittajat (2021), *Digikoulu*, https://www.yrittajat.fi/digikoulu (accessed on 22 February 2021). [39]